ONCE UPON A RHYME

IMAGINATION FOR A NEW GENERATION

Cumbria

Edited by Chris Hallam

 Young**Writers**

First published in Great Britain in 2004 by:
Young Writers
Remus House
Coltsfoot Drive
Peterborough
PE2 9JX
Telephone: 01733 890066
Website: www.youngwriters.co.uk

SB ISBN 1 84460 468 3

Foreword

Young Writers was established in 1991 and has been passionately devoted to the promotion of reading and writing in children and young adults ever since. The quest continues today. Young Writers remains as committed to engendering the fostering of burgeoning poetic and literary talent as ever.

This year's Young Writers competition has proven as vibrant and dynamic as ever and we are delighted to present a showcase of the best poetry from across the UK. Each poem has been carefully selected from a wealth of *Once Upon A Rhyme* entries before ultimately being published in this, our twelfth primary school poetry series.

Once again, we have been supremely impressed by the overall high quality of the entries we have received. The imagination, energy and creativity which has gone into each young writer's entry made choosing the best poems a challenging and often difficult but ultimately hugely rewarding task - the general high standard of the work submitted amply vindicating this opportunity to bring their poetry to a larger appreciative audience.

We sincerely hope you are pleased with our final selection and that you will enjoy *Once Upon A Rhyme Cumbria* for many years to come.

Contents

William Macgregor (9)	24
Hannah Farrell (8)	24
Nerea Bradbury (10)	25
Pui Yu Liu (9)	25
Laura Wisdom (10)	26
Alice Murray (9)	26
Grace Harrison (8)	27
Cameron Leigh (8)	27
Helena Wilson (9)	28
Laura Stobbs (9)	28
Kate McNulty (10)	29
Ben Stacey (10)	29
Grace Williams (10)	30
Grace Jamieson (8)	30

Bolton CE Primary School

Kate Brown (10)	31
Rachael Evans (9)	31
Katrina Evans (11)	32
Lauren Milburn (9)	32
Daniel Ewart (10)	33
Joanne Holliday (10)	33
Kayleigh Stalker (11)	34
Rosie Thompson (10)	34
Laura Swan (11)	35
Paul Gale (10)	35
Rebecca Jefferson (10)	36
Harry Twentyman (10)	36
Emily Ovens (10)	37
Andrew Pearson (9)	37
Laurie Paterson (10)	37
James Huntington (11)	37
Emma Pearson (11)	38
Sophie Riddick (10)	38
James Routledge (11)	38
Simon Smith (11)	38

Burton Morewood School

Charlotte Dewhirst (10)	39
Alexander Hill (10)	40
Mark Chaffer (10)	41

Crosby-On-Eden CE Primary School

Dean Barwick Primary School

Megan McTiernan (9)	68
Akiko Smith (8)	69
David Lenihan (10)	69
Caroline Walker (11)	69
Abby Fry (9)	70
Michelle Jackson (10)	70
Nina Bownass (9)	71
Emily Park (9)	71
George Willard (9)	72
Abby Cook (10)	72

Gosforth CE Primary School

Jamie O'Donnell (9)	72
Ashleigh Orrell (11)	73
Denise Naylor (10)	73
Chris Simpson (10)	74
Emily Mitchell (10)	74
Laura Slater (9)	74
Casey Blanchard (11)	75
Zoe Potter (10)	75
Class 3	76
Nicole Trainor (10)	77
Hannah Skeen (10)	78

Grayrigg CE Primary School

Charlotte Knowles (9)	79
Robin Littlewood (11)	79
Lucy Kelly (8)	80
Josie Gledhill (10)	80
Joe Clement (8)	80
Henry Knowles (11)	81
Shahra Halstead (8)	81
Stephen Park (10)	81
Bryoni Holland (9)	82
Oliver Philpott-Smith (10)	82

Greengate Junior School

Cariss Instance (10)	83
Laura Reid (10)	83

Liam Flynn (11)	84
Kirsty Bagshaw (10)	84
Rhys Studt (10)	84
Scott Reynolds (11)	85
Steven Dominik Coleman (11)	85
Charlotte Benson (10)	85
Kirsty Kneale (11)	86
Michael Turnbull (10)	86
Nicola Dunstan (11)	87
John Blain (11)	87

Heversham St Peter's CE Primary School

Thomas Davies (10)	88
Jack Graham (8)	88
Holly Robinson (9)	89
Leah Rushton (8)	89
Sophie Richards (7)	90
Alex Child (8)	90
Alex Hyman (7)	91
Robert McFadden (7)	91
Zak Crosby-McCann (7)	92
Ben Robinson (7)	92
Alice Pickthall (9)	93
Eilish McDougall (9)	94
Emma Handley (8)	94
Katie Dootson (7)	95
Jamie Dootson (10)	95
Sarah Garnett (7)	96
Rosanna Ely (8)	96
Sophie Fishwick (10)	97
Kimberley Nelson (7)	97
Jack Kerr (9)	98
Natasha Wightman (8)	98
Samuel Willacy (10)	99
William McFadden (10)	99
Amy Fox (8)	100

High Hesket Primary School

Daniel Butterworth (8)	100
Megan Norwood (8)	101
Dawn Gibson (8)	102

Connie Wainwright (9)   102
Laura Atkinson (8)   103
Victoria Armstrong (9)   103
Jade Robley (8)   103
Matthew Usher (8)   104
Jamie Foster (8)   104
Tabitha Clark (7)   105
Josh Brown (8)   105
Joshua Noble (9)   105
Lucy Thomson (9)   106
Arran Johnston (8)   106
Amy Ellams (8)   107
Hannah Butterworth (7)   107
Hannah Barthel (8)   107
Joseph Dixon (8)   108
Emily Sant (7)   108
Henry Wainwright (7)   108
Jonathan Turnbull (7)   109
Robbie Sisson (8)   109
Danny Ewin (7)   109
Katie Butterworth (7)   110
Thomas Perfect (8)   110

Holy Family Catholic School

Christian Sloan (7)   110
Amy Pryer (7)   111
Patrick Allington (7)   111
Philip McArthur (7)   111
Jane Gerrard (7)   112

Ireleth St Peter's Primary School

Christopher Littlechild (9)   112
Ellysia Wallace (9)   113
Carl Hall (11)   113
Leanne Bevan (10)   114
Jamie Tyson (10)   114
Melissa Kirkby (10)   115
Daniel Tyson (11)   115
Kate Whittle (11)   116
Catherine Steele (10)   116
Sam Broadley (11)   117

Kirsten Roberts (8)   164
Joseph Fermoyle (11)   165
Laura Taylor (11)   165
Cameron Gallagher (10)   165
Kyle Dawes (10)   166
Milly Logan (9)   166
Charlotte Coote (11)   166
Philip Crompton (11)   167
William Young (11)   167
Anne-Marie White (10)   167
Alice Barnes (9)   168
Gemma Brown (10)   168
Matthew Pickering (11)   169
Samuel Clayton (10)   169

Seascale Primary School
Joe Herbert (11)   169
Louise Smith (11)   170
Sarah Huddleston (11)   170
Katie Linington (11)   170
Sadie Skivington (9)   170
Georgia Armstrong (10)   171
Rachel Borwick (11)   171
Kellie Walker (11)   171
Nathan Clark (9)   171
Sarah White (9)   172
Matthew Thomas (11)   172
Luke McKerrow (9)   172
Peter Maxim (9)   173
Katie Dorward (9)   173
Lauren MacGregor (10)   173
Michael Krukowski (9)   174
Terrence Fail (10)   174
Daniel McKerrow (11)   174
Thomas Jordan (9)   175
Ryan Tallentire (9)   175
Stuart Rigg (11)   175
Jane Eccles (9)   176
Jake Saunders (9)   176
Callum Grant (8)   177
Jamie Bentley (8)   177

Daniel Yetts (9)	178
Luke Franks (9)	178
Lauren Oaten (8)	179
Nathan Rooney (9)	179
Abbie N'Gale-Carrington (8)	179

Sedbergh Primary School

Eilidh Sproul (8)	180
Bethany Orr (8)	180
Amy Bolsher (8)	180
Edward Pike (8)	181
Zoe Jones (9)	181
Thomas Rosenzweig (9)	181
Natalie Milburn (9)	182
Matty Goad (8)	182
Adam Roberts (8)	183
Izaak Tyson-Hirst (9)	183
Simon Hunter (9)	183
Emma Postlethwaite (9)	184
Amy Thompson (9)	184
Kristina Armitstead (9)	184
Laura Woodfine (8)	185
Tom Cooling (9)	185
Lewis Harrison (9)	185

Warcop CE Primary School

Hannah Stringer (9)	186
Bethany White (11)	186
Chelsea Venning (10)	187
Sam Pearson (10)	187
Hannah Hodgson (9)	187
Elizabeth Koronka (10)	188
Katie Bousfield (9)	188
Robert Shannon (11)	188
Kate Hayllar (11)	189
Nikki Hughes (10)	189
Thomas Balmer (10)	189
Tom Ellis (10)	190
Magan Simpson (10)	190
Lauren Holmes (9)	190

Windermere Junior School

Luke Parry (11)	191
Kerri Hird (10)	192
Megan Dean (11)	192
Katrina Sheehan (11)	192
Alex Marsden (10)	193
Charlotte Wragg (10)	193
Charlie Cook (10)	194
Joshua Bateson (11)	195
Eilish Heatley (11)	195
Romilly Calvert (10)	196
Vanessa Sanderson (9)	196
Marcus Bell (9)	197
William Williamson (9)	197
Abigail Kendrick (10)	198
Chris Black (10)	198

The Poems

McDonald's

Delicious cheeseburger in a bun,
Freshly cooked fries with a piece of roll,
A tub of ketchup with all that,
To finish it off, a little fat.

Another Big Mac,
With extra large fries,
To go with all that,
Maybe another tub of ketchup.

Fresh fruit in a little packet,
Some apples all red skin
And some grapes all green and red,
Gobble, gobble, all gone.

Chocolate, crunchy and Smarties,
All in fresh ice cream,
Chocolate sprinkles,
All mixed together.

The ultimate meal.

Dai-Anne Davidson (10)
Austin Friars St Monica's School

Autumn

The leaves fall from the trees,
The wind blows high
And lots of conkers are falling from the sky.
Now let's get a rake to sweep up all the leaves,
Make a pile of them to jump in.
Now let's collect conkers that have fallen on the ground,
Look at all the coloured leaves.
Now we will go inside,
So let's go home.

Ellen Jardine (8)
Austin Friars St Monica's School

Arctic Animals

The polar bear is so big and white
He goes hunting through the night
He has big claws to dig and hunt
They never break or go blunt

The penguin is very big and tall
You can hear his loud call
He has webbed feet to help him swim
On the end of his muscular limb

The snow rabbit is small and white
He covers up in snow to keep out of sight
He can leap a metre at a time
Always jumping in a straight line

Arctic animals are so sweet
Don't go near them you'll end up as meat
They have thick fur to keep them warm
Stay away from them you've been warned.

Georgia Routledge (10)
Austin Friars St Monica's School

Life

How does it feel to be alive?
What are living things?
Animals are alive just like you and me.

Animals are jumping, people running by,
Lots of different actions, even for a fly.

Lots of pictures are the same,
Maybe snowflakes too,
But all of us are different,
Even me and you.

But what about when I'm dead and gone?
Would you still love me? Would anyone?
'I'll always love you,' said my mum,
'I'll never stop doing it even for everyone.'

Loren Ewart (7)
Austin Friars St Monica's School

The Haunted Mansion

Up in the attic it's very dramatic,
The tension is rising, there could be something very surprising,
I'm opening the curtain, here it comes, here it comes,
What's that in the shower? It's Dracula scratching his bum.

Down in the musky, dusty basement,
A zombie was lying there fast asleep
And a dusty floor which needed a sweep.

In the middle of the floor dancing and prancing,
We're ghosts having a karaoke, it was so enchanting,
But then suddenly the music went off,
It was the zombie so annoyed with all the loud racket and noise.

You'll never believe it outside, outside,
It's the witches flying high
Among the stars in that deep blue sky.

But we can't forget outside in the garden,
The skeletons are begging the Rottweillers' pardon,
Standing there in their crowds,
Unlike the others not being that loud.

What a *haunted mansion* this place is,
Ghosts flying along the hallway to and fro,
You'd better watch out or they'll get you, you know!

Bianca Errigo (11)
Austin Friars St Monica's School

Kittens

Kittens are so soft and cuddly.
I like to cuddle them so much.
If I had a kitten I would cuddle it at night.
I would call it Jess if it was a girl.
If it was a boy I would call it Eric.

Lucy Ioannou (7)
Austin Friars St Monica's School

Swordfish Stew

I was swimming in the sea
I was stung by a bee
I screamed in pain and felt a flea
I scratched my back it attracted
A rat which jumped on my float.

Down down down
I went to the sea
I found some tangled cutlery
I saw a swordfish floating about
It gave me a shock
Which made me land on a crocodile's back.

Along came a hammerhead
He went to the loo
And ate a rat or two.

I smashed the swordfish up to stew,
Watch out he's after you too!

Daniel Alberti (8)
Austin Friars St Monica's School

I Like Animals

I like monkeys swinging high
Reaching up towards the sky.
Eating, playing, having fun
Jumping around in the sun.

I like elephants big and strong
Working hard, all day long,
Pushing here and pulling there
You can see them everywhere.

I like dogs best of all
Playing catch with a ball,
They like to roll all around
And make a mess on the ground.

Rachel Park (10)
Austin Friars St Monica's School

Valentine's Day

Valentine's day's coming soon
Five or six days away
Will I get a card?
Will I send a card?
Let me see.

Will it be roses
One dozen in a bouquet
A meal or chocolate,
Let's wait and see!

Choose a card.
Too many to choose from.
Yes this one here,
Now sign with a big '?'
And XXX.

The day is here,
Will I get one back?
Yes, yes, yes!
Signed with a kiss
Who sent it?

Zoe Forbes (11)
Austin Friars St Monica's School

He Can Do It

He can talk the talk,
He can walk the walk,
He can talk the walk.

He can run at the speed of light,
He can fly like a plane,
He can turn like a roundabout.

He can dig like a dog,
He can swim like a shark,
He can jump to sweet Heaven.

Angelo Errigo (7)
Austin Friars St Monica's School

Words Can Mean More Than They Seem

I'm reading a book
I'm having a look,
Into a world,
Where every cranny and nook,
Is filled with excitement,
Laughter and joy,
Sorrowful tears,
No cares could destroy!

Look at the creatures,
Such alien features,
Here there's no need,
For any kind of teachers,
I'm free to explore,
Adventures galore,
You'd think that's enough,
But no there's more!

Technology's thriving,
Information's driving,
This world by itself,
The story's now diving,
Into a hole,
It cannot escape,
The tension is rising,
I just can't wait!

I'll finish this story,
No matter how gory,
No matter how sad,
No matter how boring,
Three pages to go,
A journey through snow,
Through fire and fright,
Cool waters, that's right!

I've read it,
I said it,
Give the author
Some credit,
I've turned the last page,
Of that cliffhanger tale,
So I'm off to the book store,
To see what's on sale!

Elizabeth Potter (11)
Austin Friars St Monica's School

Skiing

Go skiing with a scoosh,
No time for a whoosh,
After soaring off a cornice,
You land and turn corners,
You're skiing,
As free as a bird.

It's time to stop for lunch,
To pack up more punch,
For later in the day,
When you'll make snowboarders pay,
You're skiing,
As free as a bird.

Wild skiing that's the game
And yodelling as if insane,
With your headband and goggles
And maybe some toggles,
You're skiing,
As free as a bird.

Angus Sloan (11)
Austin Friars St Monica's School

The Dream Holiday

Hullabaloo! Hullabaloo!
Everything's Hullabaloo!
It's a Saturday afternoon
And everything's Hullabaloo!
We're packing for our holiday,
The neighbours are packing too,
Because it's the summer holidays
And everything's Hullabaloo!

Commotion! Commotion!
Everything's a commotion!
My mum's forgotten the lotion
And everything's a commotion!
We're now at the airport,
Nothing is in motion,
We're sleeping at the airport
And everything's a commotion!

Rush! Rush!
Everything's a rush!
Thomas Cook
Are beating about the bush,
It wasn't planned to be like this,
The aeroplane food is like mush,
We're on the plane to Malaga
And everything is a rush!

Quiet! Quiet!
Everything's so quiet!
I'm sleeping in my bed at home,
My dad is on a diet,
I can hear him raiding the fridge at night,
(Apart from that),
Everything's so quiet!

Dream! Dream!
Everything was a dream!
I was sunbathing in Malaga,
Licking my ice cream,
But everything was a dream!
I've just been dragged right out of bed
And hit my head on the beam,
There's really nothing to be said,
Cos everything was a dream!

Fay Codona (10)
Austin Friars St Monica's School

The Hawk

The hawk is an alert, sharp minded creature,
Its eyes inspect all the surroundings.
When he's ready to go he leaps in the air,
Going for food he finds an adventure.

Swooping down with his pointed claw,
He picks up a mouse that's filled with fright.
With a grab of his claw the mouse is dead,
He soars to a tree to eat more and more.

Ripping open his meal with a long perched beak,
He swallows it in one full gulp.
He cannot stay very long for he needs to go,
For more food he needs to seek.

With a flap of his wing he's out of the lane,
His widespread wings take off.
His call is a signal that he is coming,
But we will never see him again.

Emma Johnston (10)
Austin Friars St Monica's School

Animals

Animals are cute,
Big and small,
Some are fat,
Some are tall,
But I like cats,
They are the best,
Stripy, spotty,
I don't care.

I don't mind rabbits,
But they sometimes scratch
And they are kept in a hutch,
I think that's rather sad.
If I had a rabbit,
I would love it to bits
And play with it
And feed it,
Every day.

Katie Marie Maddison (10)
Austin Friars St Monica's School

Weather

It's cold outside
With the howling winds.

Snow sledges
And snowball fights.

Some fresh air
The sun is out.

Playing in the park
All the way too dark.

Oh no it's raining
I forgot my umbrella.

Natalie Smith (10)
Austin Friars St Monica's School

My Gran

My grandma's mad
She's not all wrinkled up and sad
She runs around playing tig
Not like the others, their exercise
Is putting on their wig.

One day she was taken away
She was no longer able to play
And no longer was she free to roam
She was put in the high tower
Of a retirement home.

She was put under a curse
By the evil nurse
This big ugly man in a long white coat
Told my grandma not to smoke
She tried, but carried on and died

We went to the funeral
To build up morale
And Dad said I was very brave
It's a shame, I thought
As she went off to the grave

This is the end of my granny
It's also the end of my story
So I'll see you next time
When I've thought up another rhyme.

Elliot Watson (11)
Austin Friars St Monica's School

The Rugby Match

It was like a battlefield,
With guns and mortars sounding.
The players diving in like stukas,
And the coach saying, 'Just drive on.'

My friend who was called Alex,
Dived over for our first try.
Our forward, Angus the Scot,
Kicked the ball in the crowd a lot.

It was just like a battlefield,
With guns and mortars sounding.
The players diving in like stukas,
And the coach saying, 'Just drive on.'

The other team's flanker called Ed,
Who had a very big head,
Grabbed the ball, gave a whoop and a call
And scored his team a try.

It was like a battlefield,
With guns and mortars sounding.
The players diving in like stukas
And the coach saying, 'Just drive on.'

Nearing the end of the match,
Jason did a catch.
Then set up a rook,
That definitely took the score to 30/5.

It was like a battlefield,
With guns and mortars sounding.
Players getting driven back
And the coach saying, 'You've done well.'

Fionntán Lawlor (10)
Austin Friars St Monica's School

Mice And Cats

I'm a little mouse in a house,
Under the ground and all around,
Eating cheese it makes me sneeze.

Going down it makes me frown,
Getting food it is so good,
Mice are nice they taste like spice.

Cats are unusual in all sorts of ways,
They sit around for days and days,
Staring hard into your eyes.

Wondering what happens in your lives,
Are you all different colours?
Do you pounce about trying to catch mice?

Mice and cats don't work out,
It would be rather odd,
I like them both but they mostly fight.

Lorena Christie (11)
Austin Friars St Monica's School

My Fish

My fish bubble
They bubble a lot
They are really scaly
And feel all slithery

My fish are red and orange
We clean them out every month
They like being fed
But when we put the food in
They swim to the bottom of the pond.

Jack Percival (10)
Austin Friars St Monica's School

The ATV Quad Bike Day

One day I was with my dad,
On the ATV quad bike day.
They had lots and lots of cool quad bikes,
Go-karts, they had diggers and cars.

They even had the Range Rover Freelander,
Going off road, oh it was so exciting,
Wonderful, it was probably the best day,
I have ever had in my entire life.

I wish, oh! I wish I were there right now
And I especially loved watching the quads,
As they flew off the ramp into the air.

Then I was off on my way home,
I said to my dad, I can't wait till the next,
Diggers, cars, Ranger Rovers and quads,
Next time, who knows, I'll go on my own.

Henry Lloyd (9)
Austin Friars St Monica's School

The Garden Magpie

Bold and elegant in its black and white suit,
It sits on a branch and gazes as the world goes by.
If it sees a shiny thing lying on the ground,
It swoops down to get it and uses it for a crown.

Gracefully it flies through the air
Gliding and swooping everywhere.
Over the treetops up to the clouds
Down to the garden which it surrounds
Hoping for food from a friendly face,
It's always there in the same place.

It perches on branches that sway in the wind,
It waits patiently for its mate to come down to him.
Together they sing a delightful song
And they feel happy where they belong.

Jamie Johnston (10)
Austin Friars St Monica's School

My Life

The people that are important to me are
Family, friends and Mr B,
They're caring, kind and helpful to just me.

School and church are a different
Experience to me they help you learn
And walk the way God wants.

But reading is important to me
Because I enjoy it really
I do it for fun, you should like it too.

I enjoy horse riding, swimming and netball too,
But I ask myself, 'Why is it fun?' I said to myself,
It's fun because I enjoy it.

My dogs Ollie and Poppy are important to me
But Poppy is quite a stroppy dog
She messes up and runs off with our slippers
But I do love them.

My mum is a sweet person, I love her very much
When she's not there I don't know what to do
I love her as much as I can when she's there.

My sister is a cheeky little girl
When she squeaks instead
She says that she doesn't love me
But she really does.

Mr B my teacher is really funny,
I like my teacher, he's really kind
When he tells a joke everyone laughs
Because it's so funny, it's someone's life.

Charlotte Elizabeth Ann Scott (10)
Austin Friars St Monica's School

My Week

Monday it starts off in the morning all week long,
I watch TV then I go to school at eight o'clock,
It is a long day at school till quarter to four,
Then I go to Grandma's to have tea, I also watch a bit of TV.
At five o'clock I go home to do my homework.
Then have three games of chess with Dad, then straight to bed.

Tuesday I go to school at the same time
But this time for homework it is mental arithmetic
When school ends it is back to Grandma's for tea,
Then from 6pm to 7pm I go to city of Carlisle swimming club
Then we go home, I do my homework.
When I have finished my homework I go to bed.

Wednesday on the way to school I listen to my favourite song
On the radio,
After school I go to chess until 5pm, then I go to tennis till 6pm,
Then I go home, do my homework and play on my PlayStation 2
For a while, go to bed and to sleep.

Thursday at school in the morning normally have maths numbers
And often maths number.
It is playtime, we sometimes play tig, at 3pm we play rugby or football,
After school I go straight to City of Carlisle swimming club
Then I go home to do my homework and go to bed.

Friday in the morning I listen to my favourite song again after school,
I got to go to football after school I go to swimming at St Aidan's
from 6pm to 7pm,
I get a McDonald's, go home and I have all that free time to play
a game called Rummikub and I win every game.

Paul Adam van Iterson (10)
Austin Friars St Monica's School

The Beach

Walking to the beach and smelling the sea air,
Walking to the beach we're nearly, nearly there.
Step on to the sand and feel it between your toes,
Touch it with your hand, don't get it up your nose.
Get your wet suit on and run towards the sea,
Our belly boards my sister and me.

Swimming to where the waves break,
Now we've only got to wait.
Here comes a big wave, hop on your belly board,
Don't forget to grab hold of the cord.
My sister and me get swept onto the shore,
That was fun! Let's do it once more!

Let's put some suncream on,
The sun is getting bright.
Factor 20 please, or I'll itch all night.
I'll rub it on you and you rub it on me,
But do it again if you go in the sea.

Let's build a sandcastle,
Ellen gets the water from the sea.
I'll get the sand hee hee hee!
But once we've made it we'll have to go,
But I'll see the beach tomorrow though.

Harriet Jardine (10)
Austin Friars St Monica's School

Dolphinduck

Dolphin swims through the sea
With its duck's feet.
Splish splash with its feet.
It does not know when he got them.
We think he got them from a puddle
Or in a river or the sea.
Do you know where he got them?

Natalie Forbes (9)
Austin Friars St Monica's School

Food

Food, food it's very very nice,
Keeps me asleep all night,
Thick porridge for breakfast
With bananas and milk,
I love them all because they're very tasty.

I ask my mum what's for lunch,
She said crispy bacon and sizzling sausages,
So lovely and juicy they all are,
They tumble down my mouth in one big gulp.

I come downstairs to see what's for dinner,
It's thin, crispy margerita pizza,
So cheesy and tasty it's very very nice
It trickles down my mouth in one big slice.

I end my poem to say food, food is very nice,
But my favourite has got to be rice,
As I go upstairs to my bed to sleep,
I wonder what's on the menu next week?

Saathvik Shetty (10)
Austin Friars St Monica's School

My Birthday

I'm happy, I'm happy, let's celebrate,
It's my birthday and I have just turned eight,
We're having a party, my friends and me,
We're going to eat cakes and jelly for tea.

My party's a disco with dancing and games,
We're having a karaoke, I think that's its name,
I will sing Atomic Kitten at the top of my voice,
Everyone will listen, they won't have a choice!

My presents were wrapped all shiny and fine,
I can't wait until next year when I will be nine!

Joanna Kennell (8)
Austin Friars St Monica's School

What's Important To Me

I love to play football, rugby, cricket in my garden,
I like it when my family and friends come round to play,
I liked it when we went on holiday to Spain,
With all our friends it was good fun playing in the sea.

I was very happy when Jimmy Glass scored for Carlisle,
We had stayed in the league we all ran onto the pitch,
I liked it when I got a tour round the Millennium stadium,
It was a lot of fun watching Carlisle at the Millennium stadium.

I love going to watch cricket matches and getting autographs,
I like going to play cricket at Millom and in my garden.
It was great fun practising my leg spin bowling at Manchester,
It was great when I had a cricket party for my birthday.

It was good fun going to watch rugby matches with my dad,
I like going to rugby on Monday nights after school,
I like my Newcastle Falcons top with '10 Wilkinson' on the back,
I like playing rugby in my garden with my brother.

Nicholas Watt (9)
Austin Friars St Monica's School

Football Number One

I tried to pass
But the ball went in the glass.

I tried to do a header,
But I kept going redder,
I am a good leaper which
Makes me a good keeper.

Football is one of my loves,
It all starts when I put on the gloves,
I pray to God most holy,
That I will be the best goalie.

Toby Johnston (8)
Austin Friars St Monica's School

The Football Match

We caught the bus to Man U's ground
And there was an outrageous sound.
As the team pulled up outside,
The stadium that's tall and wide.

Our team was at the top of the table
And I thought that they were able,
To beat the team they were playing
And keep the commentators saying, *goal!*

We got some snacks, went to our seats
And said it would be an amazing feat
If the other team were to beat
Our team that's at the top of the league.

The match started and we scored
The Man U fans stood up and roared.
We did beat them in the end
And we did send them home unhappy.

Dominic McGrath (10)
Austin Friars St Monica's School

Fireworks

Fireworks blast off into the sky,
What a bang they make,
They make my rabbit get a fright,
Fireworks are sparkly,
Bright,
Patterns that shine in your eyes,
Pink, blue, orange, green and yellow colours,
Spirals,
Circles,
People and me!

Vanessa Brown (8)
Austin Friars St Monica's School

What's Wrong With The World At The Moment?

What's wrong with the world at the moment?
People dying here and there you can see,
All of these people are dying from poverty.

There is a war in the world at the moment,
You can see it but it is hard to know it,
We're oh so, so lucky, that we have enough money.

Lots of people getting famine,
All the world can do is be damning,
How can we sleep in the world at the moment?

There are oh so many diseases,
So many people get the wheezes,
So many drugs and bad things.

There is oh so, so much pain,
All we can do is put it in vain,
How can we sleep in the world at the moment?

Alex W Rheinbach (10)
Austin Friars St Monica's School

Birthday

Happy birthday to me.
I am going to have a party.
All my classmates are invited.
I will have balloons.
Jelly eaten with spoons.
Cakes with candles to blow out
Because on your birthday
A wish is what it's all about.
Hope you can all come
To join in all the fun.

Sam Groom (8)
Austin Friars St Monica's School

My Favourite Sports

My favourite sports are football and rugby, they are fun,
When I played my first game oh it was fun,
My first goal oh how it was good, better than the rest,
When I was in goal I was scared but I did not let one in.

When I played my first rugby match it was fun,
I have not scored a try yet, it is still fun,
It is cold when we are waiting to go onto the pitch,
After we have played the games we are covered head to foot in mud.

Fishing is fun, I go when it is hot or cold,
When the river is fast flowing or is running slow,
There are big fish and small fish in the river,
If the river is high or low it is still fun.

All the sports I do they are fun,
What I enjoy about football is the taking part,
Fishing is fun because you can eat the fish when you catch them,
Rugby is fun because you can dump-tackle people.

Alex Peart (10)
Austin Friars St Monica's School

Daisy The Hard-Backed Fish

I had a fish her name was Daisy,
She was half fish half turtle,
She looked rather crazy.
She swam around upside down
With her fins, she spun round and round.
She always swam the wrong way round,
What a silly fish!
Daisy was a silly thing,
She really loved to swim.
What a silly fish!

Nicola McKenzie (8)
Austin Friars St Monica's School

My Dreams

This may seem a dream,
But it is a team,
Of my ideas,
Through my life.

My bedroom is not a room with a bed in it,
It is a room of thoughts that have been lit,
My music, my figures, my thoughts and dreams,
This may be a dream but it is a team.

I dream I am playing against my teacher in a chess match
And win that match,
I dream I'm playing a match for Manchester United,
Against Man City in the FA Cup.

I swim for Scotland against America
And win the trophy and take it home.
My imagination how nice it is,
I don't believe it's so nice.

A team of thoughts,
It's not a dream,
It is a team
Of my life.

Jack Alexander Stephenson (10)
Austin Friars St Monica's School

Hallowe'en Witches

Witches in Hallowe'en are funny and loud but . . .
I think cats and ghosts are better,
I think cats are black and witches are wicked
And I wonder what is going to happen next.

Samantha Christie (9)
Austin Friars St Monica's School

Bikes

I like bikes, small and fast,
I like bikes, bound to last,
Some are black, some are blue,
Some bikes cost quite a few.

I like bikes with some gears,
I like bikes, which last some years,
Some are big, some are small,
Some bike shops, make their prices fall.

I like my bike, nice and safe,
I ride my bike in a safe place,
I ride my bike in the garden,
Bump into Mum, 'I beg your pardon.'

I like my bike, it's red and green
And it's got gears of eighteen,
Its name is free spirit,
A lovely bike with a lovely spirit.

William Macgregor (9)
Austin Friars St Monica's School

That Noise

That noise in my bedroom,
It creaks every night.
I saw it on Monday,
Oh what a big fright!

It's slimy and green
With big bold blue eyes,
I hid under my pillow
And what a surprise!

He was standing there
Blood from his mouth,
I screamed so loud
The people down south,
Could hear my shout no doubt!

Hannah Farrell (8)
Austin Friars St Monica's School

My Life

At school I like to see my friends,
At home I like to see my dog,
When I'm at school I don't like stories,
But in the end I love to read.

At Christmas I like to see my friends,
At parties I love to see my family,
On Saturday I play with my dog and cat,
On Sunday I go to church for an hour.

Then it's the beginning of a new week,
We have history today, oh yes my favourite,
Then we have English, oh no it's awful,
Then it's . . . Spanish, oh well, not my best day!

All of a sudden it comes, Friday's here,
We all work extra hard, we do RE,
We do ICT then it's hometime,
It's been a great week. It really has.

Nerea Bradbury (10)
Austin Friars St Monica's School

Swans In The Lake

Swans swimming in the lake,
White feathers in the long lake,
Drift along the blue lake
And higher and higher,
Fly and fly and fly.

And down and down and down,
And drift and drift and drift,
And swim through the long lake once again,
And fly away until another day.

Pui Yu Liu (9)
Austin Friars St Monica's School

My Pet Hamster Bill

Bill, Bill never gets ill,
Still he chews wood, pencils and rulers.
He's asleep in the light
And awake in the night,
That's Bill, Bill, Bill.

Bill is speedier than a mouse,
On his lead and in his house.
He rolls and rolls in his ball,
All along and round the hall.
Bill runs in his wheel eight miles every night,
Then goes to bed in the light.

Bill lives on his own in his metal cage,
He hasn't had his first birthday yet,
But he's already beginning to age,
He's big and furry all cuddly and soft,
His eyes are all black and bright,
But when you hold him he can bite.

Bill, Bill loves food,
Even if it's green and disgusting.
He'll eat anything,
He can get his hands on,
But there's no one like Bill,
He's Bill my cool furry hamster.

Laura Wisdom (10)
Austin Friars St Monica's School

If I Was A Cat

If I was a cat I'd jump through the trees,
I'd run past the rabbits onto the leaves,
I'd pounce on the mice so I'd eat them for dinner,
I'd run back to the river, back to my home
And perch on the chair and sleep in the sun.

Alice Murray (9)
Austin Friars St Monica's School

The Everything Giraffe

Once there was a giraffe
Who lived far far away
In a magical place
Called the wish motorway.

She wanted to be everything
But didn't know what to choose?
Suddenly there was a flash from her feet.
There appeared some trainer shoes.

In the next two hours
She had wings from a bird,
Ears of a cat, horns from a goat
And tail of a rat.

Teeth of a dinosaur,
Legs from a dog,
Muscles from a tiger
And tongue of a frog.

In three minutes
It was even worse!
Fin of a shark
And just about to burst!

Grace Harrison (8)
Austin Friars St Monica's School

Dolphins

Dolphins, glamorous dolphins swimming through the night,
With the guidance of the moon,
Jumping along as well,
Smiling happily, water coming out of their blow hole,
Playing along in the sea,
Oh how I wish I could swim along with the dolphins!

Cameron Leigh (8)
Austin Friars St Monica's School

My Life

My family takes the leading role,
As important things to my soul.
At the turn of each tide,
They are there at my side,
Oh, what would I do without them?

Animals are the second step to this brilliant life of mine
And looking after my pet cats takes up much of my time.
Horses are important to me,
Without them where would I be?
There is nothing like sailing round the ring hearing the applause
of the crowd.

On a wild windy evening,
You will usually find me reading.
Curling up with a book,
While your mother does cook,
It is a very cosy feeling.

My school is an excellent school
And my teacher is so cool.
At the end of the day,
I go out and play,
On my bike in my wonderful garden.

Helena Wilson (9)
Austin Friars St Monica's School

Bonfire Night

Bonfire Night,
What a wonderful sight,
Watching rockets and fires
Made of gunpowder and tyres.

The night sky lights up,
While I sip from my cup,
As fireworks explode in the sky
I drink tea and toast 'Guy'.

Laura Stobbs (9)
Austin Friars St Monica's School

The Mountains

The fresh green grass spreading for miles,
Like a long red carpet for the Queen.
Lots of fences and lots of styles,
To get to where I want to be.

When I get to the top of the mountain,
I wish there will be a water fountain,
A lot of effort and hard work, to get there in the end,
I get to the top, then the mountain's my friend.

I look around and what do I see?
A circle of mountains and then the sea,
I stay there for hours and hours looking around,
Then I get up and run back down to the ground.

The mountains so tall,
They're like a huge wall,
Some people get scared and start to get frightened,
But I know they're just friendly giants.

Kate McNulty (10)
Austin Friars St Monica's School

My Pet Guinea Pig

My pet guinea pig is called Charlie, he's cute,
He plays with his box, he likes to knock it over
And he jumps up and down from his box.

He likes to steal the rabbit's food from the rabbits,
Then he buries them in the hay in the hutch.
The rabbits then try and get it back.

In the summer my guinea pig gets put out,
In an outside hutch, he jumps around,
He tries to escape all the time that's what he does,
When he gets put inside his hutch.

Ben Stacey (10)
Austin Friars St Monica's School

The Bee

I buzz around from flower to flower
And watch the people in the bower,
Down, down to the bottom of the garden,
Bump into a tree, 'Oh beg my pardon.'

Under the bridge I can go and fly,
Then up, up, up to the sky,
I buzz around and then fly down,
I dodge a tree and fly around.

I go up to the sky with no care at all,
Down I fly and on a toy ball,
I prepare myself, wow! I've taken off in the sky,
Fly little bee fly, fly, fly.

I fly on up to the top of a tree,
I sit, I wait, I pause not for long,
Then I start to hum a song,
So up, up to the sky,
Fly little bee fly, fly, fly.

Grace Williams (10)
Austin Friars St Monica's School

Cats

There are big cats,
There are small cats,
There are short cats
And tall cats.

There are friendly cats,
There are scary cats,
There are nice cats
And horrible cats.

There are stripy cats,
There are spotty cats,
But whatever kind they are
I love them!

Grace Jamieson (8)
Austin Friars St Monica's School

A Week Of Cumbrian Weather

(Inspired by Wes Magee)

On Monday sunshine nicely shone
But before long it had gone

Tuesday's weather was heavy rain
It dropped onto my windowpane.

Wednesday's fog was cold and damp,
Walking around with my oil lamp.

Thursday hailstones hit the ground,
As they hit I heard the sound.

Friday's wind did rage and blow,
All our spirits were very low.

Saturday's weather was cold frost
Our hopes of snow were nearly lost.

Sundays' ground was white with snow
Racing sledges go, go, go!

Kate Brown (10)
Bolton CE Primary School

Frost

The frost is a layer of glitter
Sparkling on the ground,
It is icing on a chocolate cake,
An ice cube split up,
Frost is the sugar
Sprinkled into coffee,
It is diamonds sparkling
All over the ground.
The frost is a glittering blanket
That wraps itself around the trees,
Frost is crunchy crisps
Ready to be eaten.

Rachael Evans (9)
Bolton CE Primary School

A Week Of Cumbrian Weather
(Inspired by Wes Magee)

Monday's sunshine gleamed in the skies,
But soon it said its goodbyes.

Tuesday's windows showed the rain,
Each little drop on the panes.

Wednesday's fog was dull and grey,
I wish it would just go away.

Thursday's hailstones came tumbling down,
I soon got sick of the sound.

Friday's wind made a big, bad storm,
I stayed inside to keep warm.

Saturday's frost was crisp, hard ice,
To keep us warm we had some rice.

Sunday's snow covered the ground,
Our sledge just had to be found!

Katrina Evans (11)
Bolton CE Primary School

Frost

Frost is a white sheet on your windscreen
It is crunchy crisp lying on the ground
Frost is diamonds twinkling on the grass
And the ground covered with sparkling stars
It is the icing on a wedding cake
And a blanket that wraps everything inside it.

Lauren Milburn (9)
Bolton CE Primary School

A Week Of Cumbrian Weather

(Inspired by Wes Magee)

On Monday the sun shone very bright
And I went outside to fly my kite

On Tuesday it was raining hard,
Staying inside, so I got bored.

On Wednesday I saw the thick white mist
Around my fingers it did twist.

On Thursday it was hard hailstones,
I stayed inside and really moaned.

On Friday gales blew trees down,
Causing accidents all over town.

On Saturday Jack Frost hit
And in the morning he really bit.

On Sunday we had lots of snow
And in the car we went slow.

Daniel Ewart (10)
Bolton CE Primary School

Wind

Wind is howling lions,
Invisible ghosts that float around picking leaves up
And dropping them again.
Wolves calling to each other through the night.
The wind is a giant breathing onto the Earth
And moving things around.
A train whistling when entering the station.

Joanne Holliday (10)
Bolton CE Primary School

A Week Of Cumbrian Weather

(Inspired by Wes Magee)

On Monday gusty wind did blow
And people moved, huddled and slow.

Tuesday's sun shone long and bright,
Warmed my face from morning to night.

Wednesday brought clouds big and dark,
Stayed at home instead of the park.

Thursday's rain falls to the grass,
Making puddles, splash, splash, splash!

Friday's hailstones fall to the ground
Breaking glass all around.

Saturday's snow blew hard and strong,
We stayed inside to sing a song.

On Sunday morning a rainbow appeared
But in the afternoon it soon disappeared.

Kayleigh Stalker (11)
Bolton CE Primary School

Thunder

Thunder is a giant beating his drum
A roaring crowd at a football match.
Thunder is an elephant, stomping through the sky,
A herd of rhinos charging at the clouds,
A building tumbling to the ground,
A bomb exploding,
A machine breaking down.
Thunder is a truck backfiring again and again.

Rosie Thompson (10)
Bolton CE Primary School

A Week Of Cumbrian Weather

(Inspired by Wes Magee)

Monday's wind blew us away,
Wind is strong, hope it doesn't stay.

Tuesday's sun was nothing but fun,
Shone in our eyes, now we're blind.

Wednesday's frost froze my toes
And gave me a bright red nose.

Thursday's snow covered the green ground
Without making a single sound.

On Friday came the cold wet rain,
Dripped on the windowpanes.

Saturday's fog covered the ground,
Nothing was seen all around.

On Sunday hailstones came and fell,
Horrid week of weather to tell.

Laura Swan (11)
Bolton CE Primary School

Thunder

Thunder is a truck starting its engine.
It is a bolt of stars coming from the sky,
A gunshot that makes us jump and
Makes the birds fly away.
A loud noise that scares us at night.
Thunder is a cannon firing in a raging battle,
A tree falling in the forest and a bomb blowing.

Paul Gale (10)
Bolton CE Primary School

A Week Of Cumbrian Weather
(Inspired by Wes Magee)

On Monday the sun shone bright
Walked my dog in the dazzling light.

Tuesday it was pouring down
Trickling water all over town.

On Wednesday fog was wet and damp
Walking around with my oil lamp.

Thursday hailstones crashed and bashed
While the lightning started to flash.

Friday's wind blew hard and strong
Gusted hard all morning long.

On Saturday Jack Frost came
Sat inside playing a game.

Sunday's snow was cold and breezy
Made my throat go dry and wheezy.

Rebecca Jefferson (10)
Bolton CE Primary School

Lightning

Lightning is a shooting star
Disco light for the birds
Lightning is a blond streak in your dark hair
Neon light flashing on and off in the city streets
A knife blade glinting in the light
Lightning is a bulb being switched on and off.

Harry Twentyman (10)
Bolton CE Primary School

The Sound Of Thunder

Thunder is a giant's heart thumping,
A herd of elephants running through the forest,
It is a loud drum banging,
Thunder is a robber's loud footsteps
And a jet plane close to the ground.

Emily Ovens (10)
Bolton CE Primary School

Thunder

Thunder is the rhythmic beat on drums
It is a herd of stampeding elephants
It is two giants fighting, swinging their clubs at each other
Thunder is a heavy box dropped from a height
It is the thud of trees falling.

Andrew Pearson (9)
Bolton CE Primary School

Wild Cat

A beast with eyes of water.
Fur like silk.
The teeth are pins that stab and pierce.
He slips away like a snake slithering to catch its prey.

Laurie Paterson (10)
Bolton CE Primary School

Wild Cat

A beast with eyes of burning fire.
Fur like barbed wire.
The teeth of a rough Aztec knife.
He slips away like a snake.

James Huntington (11)
Bolton CE Primary School

Mist

Mist is a woolly jumper that has been in the rain.
Fog is an invisible hand creeping down my back.
It is a concrete wall that you can't see or walk through.
Damp cotton wool that keeps out the sun,
Mist is a passage of smoke to make you get lost.
A giant's wife sieving flour to make a cake.

Emma Pearson (11)
Bolton CE Primary School

Clouds

A cloud is a sheep running across the sky.
It is a bag of cotton wool.
A grey cloak wrapped around
The sun hiding the sunlight
They are bubbles floating in my nice bath.
Clouds are marshmallows on hot chocolate.

Sophie Riddick (10)
Bolton CE Primary School

The Wild Cat

A beast with eyes of glittering emeralds,
Fur as rough as a rock,
The teeth are small daggers,
He slips away, as quiet as a mouse.

James Routledge (11)
Bolton CE Primary School

Haiku

I like art a lot
I like playing and writing
I think school is cool.

Simon Smith (11)
Bolton CE Primary School

I'm Up A Mountain

I'm up a mountain,
A high mountain,
The mist is thick,
I can barely pick up my feet.

Though the mist is thick,
The wind still howls,
It's loud, so loud on the mountain top,
I feel as though I'm going to pop.

The mist is still thick,
The wind still howls and roars,
But now I've reached the crevice,
So scary and deep,
So steep, I nearly weep.

The mist is thick,
The wind still howls,
And I've passed the crevice,

And now the snow is deep,
It's crispy in and soft out,
I'm sinking in I need to shout!

The mist still grows,
The mist still howls and growls,
And that was the last crevice,

The snow still deep,
But argh! an avalanche,
It's rumbling,
It's tumbling,
It's going the other way!

The mist is thick,
The wind still roars,
No more crevice,
No more deep snow,
The avalanche has gone.

Charlotte Dewhirst (10)
Burton Morewood School

Autumn

Frost making patterns on the leaves,
With little tiny ice crystals,
Resting on the trees
And the frost kept on growing.
Dew on a spider's web,
Dazzlingly bright,
But if no light is shining,
It's sure to give you a fright,
for it will stick to your body,
While the dews on the spider's web,
Kept on twinkling.
The hedgehogs sleeping in the leaves,
The squirrels zooming through the trees,
Trying to find rest,
to do as they please
And the animals kept on sleeping.
Now for the leaves,
Which were golden on the trees,
But now are brown, on the ground,
With sycamore seeds twirling around
And the leaves kept falling down.
And finally for the trees,
Some bare, some colourful,
Most with swaying branches,
Swaying from side to side,
And all these things kept on happening.

Alexander Hill (10)
Burton Morewood School

Everest

As we set off,
From tent ridden base camp,
We began to notice
The cold and the damp.

Then we went higher,
Higher and higher,
We said snowflakes were harmless,
But then we were liars.

Then that night
A blizzard blew up,
It left us stood staring
At a cold icy dump.

The time we stayed
For a week at high camp
Playing chess by the light
Of a small oil lamp.

Then five days later
We reached the summit
I pretended to be scared
But really I just loved it.

Mark Chaffer (10)
Burton Morewood School

At The Summit

Avalanche, powerful,
Racing down the mountain,
Day by day,
Climbers trying to beat the weather.
Climbers doing their best,
To get to the summit.

Matthew Prior (11)
Burton Morewood School

Everest

E very step on Everest is hard
V enturing into dangerous ice falls
E verest claims many lives
R acing to the top before the wind blows up
E xperiments are placed up there
S afety first I always say
T otal fitness is needed here

E mpty holes called crevasses
V ery cold it is up here . . .
E xperience is vital in this cold
R eal danger lies in falls
E scape is impossible from a crevasse
S imply the hardest mountain
T he home of the gods for Tibet.

Matthew Pickering (10)
Burton Morewood School

I Walk To My Death

There is no denying
That at least ten will die,
On a trip to the top of the world.
There's an avalanche
You can't run but you can try
And the twister
That twirled and twirled.
Climbing up Everest is like a death trap,
The crevasse disguised and deep,
We dangle up there on ropes
Above the gap
Our lives in the rope hands they keep.
Our fingers drop off
They've died, they're dead
All that I fear is
Next it might be my head.

Thomas Jackson (9)
Burton Morewood School

The Spirit Is Dying

It's trying to reach out and grab you.
It wants to take and touch your soul.
The glistening snow just isn't what it seems.
You are sure you want to do it
But then you want to run.
The roaring of the thunder is getting too much.
Help me! Help me! Just rescue me.
Hate it up here,
I want to go home but there's no one to care.

But then it all changes I don't want to go.
The sun is in my face.
There's a rumble, I know what,
Everest is taking its toll!
People have died,
Lives set aside.

When I reached the top
I am glad I stopped to see
What was up there for me,
Mountain as far as the eye could see!
Someone, *please!* Give me a hug!

Katie Prior (9)
Burton Morewood School

Avalanche

On its own it is full of wonder and ice,
Oh no! An avalanche
Is rushing down the mountain,
That's not ice!
Sliding and hurrying past,
Destroying anything in its path.
To get caught in it is like an ice cold bath.
It cannot see but it's come after me,
And I will die at last.
One tenth of people die like me,
I will be with them, not in Dundee.

Peter Hacker (10)
Burton Morewood School

Eleventh Hour

Eleventh hour of the eleventh month
On the eleventh day,
It all stopped
Nobody else had to pay,
It didn't stop the poppies' growth,
On the graves,
In the fields,
Some say look at the poppies,
But which one I ask.
Hundreds of people died
Wives, children and mums cried,
At the thought of someone
Taking another's life.
Wars are still here,
Causing people's tears,
So here we are,
Thinking about people
Who gave their lives
So brave.

Lauren Prior (9)
Burton Morewood School

Everest

Snow is falling as it can go
The wind is whistling in your ears
The snow begins to move.
I stare at the slope so deep
It starts to move
My heart begins to beat
So fast I don't think I can move.
Blizzards coming every day
Trying to blow the tents away,
An avalanche is coming
I can't move out of the way.
Now . . . I'm dead.

Emily Allen (10)
Burton Morewood School

Poppies

I'm here in my trench,
Wounded,
Left here to die,
I'm still here feeling alone
I'm cold and I'm wet,
This is no lie.

I'm still here feeling alone and scared.
I wish someone was here,
Looked after me and cared.

I'm up now on the battlefield,
Dead bodies all around,
Gunshots ringing in my ears,
I'm hating all this sound.

My mum is looking at my grave,
Poppies growing all around,
All the graves in rows,
Sinking into the ground.

Harriet Sansby (9)
Burton Morewood School

Challenge Of Everest

Every step I take, I'm risking my life,
The snowflakes are crunching
Under my feet,
I wonder where the next crevice is going to appear?
Walking up the high mountain
With the blustery wind, blowing in my face.
I suddenly see,
The avalanche thundering towards me
Down and down!
When it's passed we all get up again
But when we need water it's up to us
To get ice blocks to melt in a pan.

Lorna Looker (10)
Burton Morewood School

Walking Into Death

The wind howling when I sleep,
Rushing down the hill, ever so steep.

Coming down the hill, I hear an avalanche,
Maybe tomorrow we'll have a summit chance.

In the morning I get out of the tent,
Now we are going for a summit attempt.

We're walking up the mountain as the sun is rising,
Each step is tiring but we are not timing.

I keep saying, just ten more steps,
I could have just laid down and slept.

I want to go down but there's no way back,
I don't want to fall down a deep crevasse.

Here comes an avalanche, I'm terrified,
I can't get out the way . . .
Now I've died!

Marcus Nicholson (10)
Burton Morewood School

Nativity Poem

I wish I'd been a shepherd,
And heard the angels sing.

I wish I'd been in Bethlehem,
To see the newborn king.

I wish I'd been a wise man,
At the stable bare.

Following the star,
With gold, Frankincense and myrrh.

I wish I'd been an animal,
Who shared its manger's hay.

With that special newborn baby,
On that first Christmas day.

Rebecca Mayne (11)
Burton Morewood School

Snow Is Falling

Snow is falling
Down the hills as fast as it can go,
The wind is whistling in my ear
Along with the snow.
I stand and stare
At the slop so steep,
It begins to move
My heart takes a big leap,
It leaps so fast I think
That I will fall down.
A crevice my hope is still
As still as can be
But fainting . . . maybe.
As I am walking up I can hear
Snow falling on snow,
My dreams have come true
Whoo, whoo!

Sally Looker (9)
Burton Morewood School

The Highest Summit

The highest summit, Mount Everest
Over a hundred crevices
Very big and never-ending
Halfway up, it gets colder and colder,
Chilly and chillier,
We nearly died.
It was very, very snowy, up Mount Everest,
An avalanche, run,
Getting faster and faster,
Very high,
Unbelievable.
It was so high,
We were running out of oxygen
Nearly dying.

Sam Duckett (10)
Burton Morewood School

The Top Of The World

Everest is the top of the world,
Some people say,
It is peaceful and quiet
And some people say,
It is noisy with storms and avalanches.
People suffer clearly from frostbite
And some people live, and go to the top.
We set off out the tent,
We carried on,
We went and we went,
It was too stormy
We went back to camp
Anyway we were cold and damp.
We decided to have one last go,
I went without oxygen,
Even though I was told . . . *No! No!*
In the end it was up to me,
I did it . . .
And you wouldn't believe what I could see.
I was on top of the world.

Peter Hunt (10)
Burton Morewood School

Everest's Secrets

Upon Everest the avalanches
Are strong, lethal, deadly!

Upon Everest the snow lies white,
Soft and fragile but with secrets unknown.

Upon Everest you hear violent noises,
Down the mountainside, hurtling on their way.

Upon Everest the climate doesn't look deadly,
It is waiting for them day after day.

Upon Everest secrets are unknown.

Patrick Vicary (11)
Burton Morewood School

People

The people were hurt, but they didn't show it,
Everyone was determined,
Nothing would stop them,
People lost friends and were very caring,
But they still stayed strong.
Frostbite was dangerous,
People lost their fingers and their toes.
But it still didn't stop anybody,
They were going to do it!
People went through avalanches
Which didn't stop for days,
Everything came towards them,
But it didn't stop them,
They were going to do it!
The weather was freezing,
People wearing many layers of clothes,
Taking risks of losing everything,
They were going to do it!
And they did.

Sarah Bargh (10)
Burton Morewood School

Mount Everest

Snow is falling down the hill
As fast as it can go.
No one knowing
Where it is going to flow
Crevices, scary, dark and deep,
Crawling across the ladder, we weep.
Massive vertical faces of ice,
From the bottom, they don't look so nice.
Scenery, *excellent!*
An awesome view,
Ice everywhere,
Except on you.

Scott Brocklebank (10)
Burton Morewood School

A New Life For Me

The summer trees stood next to me,
Standing still and tall.
Their leaves shine in the summer sun,
And all mine do is fall.
A happy tree I'd like to be,
It wouldn't be that bad.
But I'm the only one that's here,
That looks extremely sad.
A colourful web of shining leaves,
That's what I had, that's what I had.

My dancing children flying round me,
As happy as can be.
Soon they'll grow up like me,
Which fills my roots with glee.
I feel the cold mid-autumn frost,
That is really bad.
The humans come and I hear a crunch,
My darlings oh how sad.
My branches swaying with my leaves,
That's what I had, that's what I had.

It's coming now, I feel it,
Without my leaves I'll freeze.
The other trees, I hear them sneeze,
And they all have their leaves.
The night grows cold over me,
And even what I had.
The trees stop the cold from reaching me,
This made me really glad.
All the webs sparkle in the sun,
That's what I had, that's what I had.

One morning I wake up,
I survived that deadly night.
I look around and the trees are bare,
All leaves out of sight.
The sun emerges from its sleep
And a sparkle from my branch I see.
A shiny web and a golden leaf,
Stare as far to see.
It's a new life for me, it's a new life for me.

Rachel Dawson (11)
Burton Morewood School

Mount Everest

Avalanches coming rumbling down the mountain,
Rampaging rocks, giant lumps of snow,
Snow and ice so cold.
Blinding me
Wind ruffling my clothes,
Up they go,
Climbing higher and higher.
Frozen toes, frozen fingers,
Sleet, snow and wind,
How will they get to the top?
Finally looking over the Himalayas,
The sun shining in my eyes,
Blinding me.
Now the climb is done.

Freya Whittaker (10)
Burton Morewood School

The Mountains

Mountains, mountains, great and tall,
But the greatest one is still to be conquered
Everest
Many try but still few survive,
You are climbing frozen to bits.
I'm watching my friends, screaming as they die,
With no warning, ice falls off the mountain
Surely they can't survive?
Now only me and Billy are still alive,
Well here comes an avalanche
He's a gonna!
Now I'm here on my own,
Not knowing what to do.
My friend Robin Hall's body lies on the ground,
I start to cry, sad to my socks,
What can I do?
Echo! Echo!
Sorry, now that's just my call.
Oh! No! Avalanche!
I shout, but then I remember,
That I'm on my own . . . *argh!*
I have been pushed down a crevice,
. . . Alone!

George McCanney (9)
Burton Morewood School

Everest, Mount Doom!

Everything peaceful and still,
No avalanches, no wind, no crevasses to fall down
Everything will change sooner or later.
The winds will start to moan
And doom itself will come.
All of a sudden,
You hear a crack or two
Then the avalanche,
Your head starts spinning,
All the horror and thoughts,
Your legs start shaking
Without further warning you're under the snow.
Crevasses to fall into
Some are hidden and some are there.
People hoping they'll survive
Another dreaded day
Hoping they won't pass away.
People getting frostbite,
People getting scared
Then a sudden feeling down your spine
Am I going to make it or am I going to die?
Then you make the top
You're worn out and you're tired
And you want to shout out to the world,
'I'm alright, I've made it!'

Carrie Ann Dobson (10)
Burton Morewood School

Upon Everest

Upon Everest
Avalanche crumble,
Roaring and crushing without warning.

Upon Everest
Frostbite strikes,
Hands, feet and toes; who knows?

Upon Everest
Howling winds
Rattling tents, all through the frosty night.

Upon Everest
Death is likely,
People crying and choppers reeling.

Miracles can happen!

James Bell (11)
Burton Morewood School

Deadly

The tallest mountain on Earth,
Blizzards, ice beams,
Thunder and snow.
People try, try and try
Cold damp, misty and fog.
Ice is reaching everywhere,
Where's the top?
Are we nearly there?
Is the mountain going to roar?
Is this the summit?
Yes, we are there!

Peter Baxendale (10)
Burton Morewood School

The Mountain

The ladders bending when you walk across the hole,
When you look down you feel all giddy,
The creaking sound when you move your feet,
Wondering just how far down it goes.
The cold wind howling round your face,
Blowing the snow off the top of the mountain,
Trying to walk through the wind is impossible.
The thick, deep snow, making your feet sink in
Every step gets harder.
You can't see a thing through the blizzard.
The avalanches rumbling in the distance,
Massive boulders rolling down the hill.
The spray going everywhere, in your eyes,
The massive amount of snow,
Falling down the mountain.
The massive rocks standing high,
The huge grey things you have to climb
The snow on the top, so slippery you can't stand.

Andrew Clarke (10)
Burton Morewood School

Avalanche

The avalanche killed these people,
One out of ten people!
English and Spanish lady climbed Mount Everest.
They made it to the top
And down again!
Crevasses deep and dark and dangerous,
People died in crevices.
Hurricane, what's that?
An avalanche coming,
Down the mountainside.
This is the end
My life is dead now.

Daniel Turner (10)
Burton Morewood School

Snowfalls

I am here on the mountain,
Going day by day meeting
Snowfalls on the way
Ducking and diving everywhere
Danger, danger, is here,
On hold is my life
Thinking of what might go wrong;
Thinking of family and friends.
Blizzards coming every day,
Bang on my face, saying to myself
I can make the top!
If I keep going day by day.
Thunder is coming down,
My heart suddenly leaps,
Big snowball coming down,
Blasting and raving.
Views and stunning mountains,
Staring, glistening,
Looking down at the snow.
I have made it to the summit.
Don't worry family,
I am coming back!

Charlotte Bunting (10)
Burton Morewood School

Snow

The snow was thundering down,
It flew, flew, flew,
The avalanche was calling
Calling for to stay.
Friends happy and hungry,
Sad and crying.
Middle camp was a glory,
Warm and heated slightly.
Crevices falling, falling far below,
Deep and scary, wide and long,
High camp, high camp,
Everywhere was scary,
Everywhere I looked.
The top is not for coming,
it will not walk towards me.
The oxygen was lacking,
My life was slipping away.
The ladder far below me
I cannot bare to look,
The lives of people,
Fell right down,
I will make it to the top.

Laura Chaldecott (11)
Burton Morewood School

The Bowling Green

We have fun taking turns
At the bowling green
With our friends
That we know

The ball is smooth
Rolling through the short grass
The shiny ball stands out really well.

It feels so calm
There's no running
So quiet . . .
And slow . . .

The people there are so skilful
They crouch down
Holding the ball
Either with finger or thumb
They always try to get near the jack.

When you roll your ball too fast
It always goes into the gutter
It sometimes gets wet when it goes in the puddles
With a *thump* on the edge of the green.

Vicky Brooks (10)
Burton Morewood School

Peak Of Glory

Avalanches crumbling,
smashing down as they fall to oblivion,
The sound so ponderous
as it ravishes down the path of death,
it is so destructive in its own way.
Winds blow indestructible
as everything in its way simply freezes
and it's never to be seen again.
The wind does what it wants,
when it wants, how it wants to do
The rocks of the sea millions of years ago
still as sharp as a needle,
as the mountain grows today,
He, the rock is covered by snow,
as he will always remain
never to be seen,
never to be seen.
The snow dazzling bright, reflecting the snow,
and melting and forming a giant river and rapids
that is to be the snow of the mountain,
that will never be inhabited.

Grant Smillie (10)
Burton Morewood School

Everest

I'm cold and tired,
I don't know what to do.
I only have Jamie,
What shall I do?

The wind whistles and howls,
All through the night.
I have to keep warm
Or I'll get frostbite.

I've heard people
Have fallen down crevices -
People reckon that
Gets you to America fast!

I heard an echo,
An avalanche at the other side
Of the mountain. I'm worried,
What lies ahead?

I'm at the summit
Of Mount Everest now.
I'm at the top of the world -
A rocky and snowy place.

Emily Byle (11)
Burton Morewood School

Mount Everest

As the avalanche flew towards me,
I ducked and dived,
I thought I could get hit
It started to get faster and faster
I didn't know what to do.
I started to panic
And I realised it can't get me.
I'm sitting in a chair!
Not climbing Mount Everest!

The crevice appeared,
I couldn't see the bottom.
It got deeper and deeper,
I thought I would fall down
I started to shake . . .
But Sally whispered, 'You're at Rheged.
Not climbing Mount Everest!'

The frosty winds were howling and whistling,
It blew me away.
'Help! I screamed
Everyone looked at me
Then I saw my friends,
Aaahhh! What a relief.

Natasha Woodend (10)
Burton Morewood School

The Summit At Last

I'm exhausted, frightened, lying in my tent,
All of us cramped trying to keep warm.
Finally morning appears,
The sparkle from the sun,
It's shining on the snow.
The snow is so thick and deep.
Then it changes from peaceful to rumbling,
An avalanche crushing, everything in its sight.
My heart stops, then beats,
The destructive rock and snow,
The howling of the wind
And the crevasses breaking.
We found safety, luckily,
But the crevices' holes were broken,
We had to use the ladders
Walking steadily, I thought of the other side.
The danger, the risks, running through my head,
The amount of equipment,
We'd all made it across.
Now the summit at last
100m, 50m, 10m the top,
the oxygen was thin,
and a view I can't describe.
We've made it at last!

Sian Irvine (10)
Burton Morewood School

The Listeners

The house stood there looking lonely,
In the darkness, at the top of the hill.
The darkness was there to take over
And the silence was there to kill!

There was no life around it,
Apart from an owl or a bat.
But then a traveller came out of the distance,
On a galloping horse he sat.

His horse came to a halt,
And the traveller started to stare.
He looked at the overgrown bushes
And at the house so deserted and bare.

He knocked on the big wooden door,
But nobody answered or came.
He knocked on the door a second time
But the same thing happened again.

So the traveller went back to where he came from,
But the same thought went through his head.
Good people used to live there
But now there are phantom listeners instead.

Sarah Tattersall (10)
Crosby-On-Eden CE Primary School

The River

Once I was a clear river,
Teeming with life and fish,
I would go back to those dear days,
If I had one wish.

I have flowed through everywhere,
Through valleys, hills and dales,
I have splashed through all weathers,
Through sun, rain and gales.

Life was good in those days,
When I flowed up and down,
I was king of the countryside,
I wore the crown.

Then that fateful day arrived,
When the machinery moved in,
They scared off my wildlife,
With their monstrous din.

The factories have destroyed me,
I'm now a murky grey,
I who have lived through good and bad,
Have been demolished today.

Children come and find me,
Though it may take a while,
You bathed in me when you were young,
But now I smell so vile.

Adults come and find me,
For I'm all in a muddle,
Smelly and polluted,
Reduced to a poisoned puddle.

Alix Thorpe (10)
Crosby-On-Eden CE Primary School

My River Tale

Once I was a playful stream,
I splished splashed through the woods,
Cascading over rocks,
That was when life was, oh so good.

I tumbled over waterfalls,
Flowing up and down,
Meandering through meadows,
Bustling with sounds.

I remember the time,
When children came to play
In my shallow waters,
Which flowed all night and day.

Then I felt things were changing,
Everything was wrong,
Birds weren't tweeting anymore
Their happy, tuneful song.

It was then I saw those factories,
They began to grow and grow,
All the life had died in me,
Horrible affects began to show.

All the plants and creatures died,
And to an open sewer I've shrunk,
And now nobody notices me,
I'm a jumble sale of junk.

Jessica Barton (10)
Crosby-On-Eden CE Primary School

On That Day

On that day
On that day,
With my auntie,
With my auntie,
We went walking in the country.

Rabbits hopping,
Birds tweeting,
Horses neighing,
Long grass swaying.

Summer smells,
Swallows darting,
Crickets singing,
Young sheep baaing.

On that day,
On that day,
With my auntie,
With my auntie.
We went walking in the country.

Dogs barking
Sun shining,
Sky blue,
It all reminds me of that day,
It all reminds me of that day.

Trees all green,
Clouds fluffy,
Breeze blowing,
Stream flowing,
Fish swimming,
Wind whispering,
It all reminds me of that day.

Louisa Nicholson (10)
Crosby-On-Eden CE Primary School

Young Writers - Once Upon A Rhyme Cumbria

The Mystery

There it was so silent
Silent and overgrown
Ivy strangled drainpipes
The house that stood alone

Its red crumbled brickwork
Cracked and shattered panes
Cobweb fringed windows
Staring out at the lanes

Then out of the distance
A traveller with his horse appeared
Their fear hardly showing
Then suddenly, the horse reared

The man ran at the house
And thumped on the door
'Let me in!' he cried
Then he fell to the floor

Emerging from the mist
Shadows appeared
They slowly crept towards him
Just as he had feared

He jumped on his horse
And galloped towards the bend
His fear left trailing
Was this the traveller's end?

Ben Spedding (9)
Crosby-On-Eden CE Primary School

I Wish

I wish you could spend one day as me,
On the lonely pavements, grey,
As the wind howls
And the cold air bites,
As I sit in the alleyway.

I wish you could spend one day as me,
Feeling hungry all the time.
As the bin lids clatter,
And the drainpipes mutter
And glittering snowflakes shine.

I wish you could spend one day as me,
With no family and no friends.
As the rain pours down
And the cars zoom past.
Hoping one day it will end.

I wish I could spend one day as you,
In a loving family home,
As I fall asleep
In my cosy bed,
I'd know I'd never be alone.

Lucy Moore (10)
Crosby-On-Eden CE Primary School

Spring Poem

Trees with sparkling buds
Lots of showers
Nearly time for newborn animals
Pretty flowers
Days getting longer, nights getting shorter
Birds tweeting in the trees.
Fairies dancing in the colourful flowers
The last of the winter winds.

Megan McTiernan (9)
Dean Barwick Primary School

Autumn

Glistening golden
Chestnut trees,
Leaves falling down
Leaves lie like a carpet.

Bare trees against deep blue skies,
Leaves turning crimson-red.
Autumn has arrived.

Fireworks exploding in
The dark black sky with
Myriads of stars.

Akiko Smith (8)
Dean Barwick Primary School

Slowly The Fog

Slowly the fog,
Glides into the wood
When you go out, you touch it.
It feels like you've put your hands through a ghost.
It battles against the sun
Change into different shapes, like a dragon
Disappears -
Nowhere to be seen!

David Lenihan (10)
Dean Barwick Primary School

Slowly The Fog

Slowly the fog
Glides along the cold ground,
Hangs in the air
Disappears then reappears
Disappears then reappears
Will it stay or will it go?

Caroline Walker (11)
Dean Barwick Primary School

Autumn Days

Glistening glossy
Chestnuts drop to the ground
Leaves like a carpet.

The sky is a-glistening
Upon the multicoloured leaves
Autumn has begun.

The sea is like steel
Dolphins swim,
Circling continuously
With glimmering gold leaves.

Abby Fry (9)
Dean Barwick Primary School

Slowly The Fog

Slowly the fog drifts
Down the yard
Into the fields
The field looks
Like white snow
Blinding and cool
Dogs barking down
The yard in the mist
No sun today
Mist and more
Mist for ever.

Michelle Jackson (10)
Dean Barwick Primary School

Every Day

Today is blue
Blue sky
Just blue

Yesterday was purple
Purple flowers
Just purple

Tomorrow will be green
Green grass
Just green

The past is grey
Dull and grey
Just grey

The future is yellow
Yellow like the sun
Just yellow.

Nina Bownass (9)
Dean Barwick Primary School

Autumn Day

Autumn is like a bare tree
Mysterious tree in the night.
Following you about at night.

It's like one flower all by
Itself, dying like a
Snowflake falling
From the sky.

Autumn is a beautiful
Bird swooping on a
Branch, playing a
Harp.

Emily Park (9)
Dean Barwick Primary School

George's Poem

I sat beneath the willow tree and saw a sweet robin
In the pond all the ducks and geese were a-bobbin.
But I had no time to sit and stare
For hungry hawks were in the air.
From little yellow buttercups on the ground
To big old oaks all around.
All these things are what I saw
That is what I wrote this for.
I also think that you will agree
The most beautiful things, are what you see.

George Willard (9)
Dean Barwick Primary School

Revenge For Mum's Broken Leg

(A true story)

Mum's broken her leg,
But it's stopped hurting now.
How did she do it?
She got sat on by a cow.
So how is the cow?
Oh! the cow's okay.
But mum reckons we
Should eat it one day.

Abby Cook (10)
Dean Barwick Primary School

My Mum - Haiku

Soft silky brown hair
Helping with lots of homework
She is my angel.

Jamie O'Donnell (9)
Gosforth CE Primary School

There's An Awful Lot Of Weirdos In Our School

There's an awful lot of weirdos in our school,
Yes, there's an awful lot of weirdos in our school!

There's a boy named Alfred Penny,
And I wish he wouldn't cry already.
There's an awful lot of weirdos in our school.

There's a girl who's big and hairy
And she's also mighty scary.
There's an awful lot of weirdos in our school.

The teacher Mrs Edgar, is frightful,
And no way is she delightful.
There's an awful lot of weirdos in our school.

As for Mrs Coverly, she's green,
And is not very lovely - or clean.
There's an awful lot of weirdos in our school.

What about Mrs James?
She's orange and scaly with a long fat taily.
There's an awful lot of weirdos in our school.

Mr Marshal is very hairy
And has a liking for scaring Mary.
There's an awful lot of weirdos in our school.

We can't forget Mr Corran, who's mad and batty
And whose favourite food is roasted ratty.
There's an awful lot of weirdos in our school.

Ashleigh Orrell (11)
Gosforth CE Primary School

The Butterfly - Haiku

Soft delicate wings,
Sucking nectar from the plants,
Fluttering back home.

Denise Naylor (10)
Gosforth CE Primary School

Bad Ending

Five days ago
I was feeling very low
Four days before
My behaviour was very poor
Three days away
I would have to pay
One day before yesterday
My troubles seemed here to stay
The day before today
I really needed to pray
Now
I'm grounded!

Chris Simpson (10)
Gosforth CE Primary School

Sadness

I feel sad when I'm happy
I cry when I'm laughing
I'm lonely with my friends
Will I ever know
Why I'm the misfit, left on my own?
Why, I'm the runt, all alone?

Emily Mitchell (10)
Gosforth CE Primary School

Country Walk

On a country walk in a very thick mist,
My girlfriend asked if I'd give her a kiss.
But I missed her lips because of the fog,
And I kissed her one-eyed dog!

Laura Slater (9)
Gosforth CE Primary School

Foxes

I like the way they freely run
I hate the horrifying tense moment
When the gun gets them

Their brilliant golden feet
Padding through the dewy grass
Not a sound to be seen or heard
Except shadows, the sun does cast

Their pounding hearts, full of joy
The sun at its lowest, casting a bronze glow
The foxes faces, gleaming
As the slender beams slip through the trees

Not long before a hunt
When the sun vanishes
Leaving the world wrapped in a black blanket
Off the foxes go for a tasty morsel

Won't be seen again till dawn.

Casey Blanchard (11)
Gosforth CE Primary School

Abandoned

Every muscle in my body is working, but my
heart, it is bleeding with sadness.
My veins are not only pumping blood, they are
also pumping anger and sorrow.
My legs are not running to win a race, they are
running away from my fears.
My voice will not talk again, it will be silent so
my ears can hear danger coming.
My nose cannot smell food, it can only smell blood.
Will I live or will I die?
I only hope the best will come.
I wish someone would find me.

Zoe Potter (10)
Gosforth CE Primary School

Class 3 Teacher's Rap

Bip bop, bip bop bap,
It's the Class 3 teachers' rap.

We all have teachers
Large and small,
We have made a rap
About them all.

Bip bop, bip bop bap,
It's the Class 3 teachers' rap.

Mrs James is gentle and kind,
She's the nicest teacher that you will ever find.
If you are in need, she's there at the double,
'Just ask for Miss, it isn't any trouble.'

Bip bop, bip bop bap,
It's the Class 3 teachers' rap.

Ms Coverley is lovely,
Her favourite lesson is poetry.
She likes good stories and loves to read,
'Just give me a book, I'll take the lead.'

Bip bop, bip bop bap,
It's the Class 3 teachers' rap.

Mr Marshall is really smart,
But he doesn't like teaching 'arty clart'
Mr Marshall loves teaching his class,
Just keep him away from balls and glass!

Bip bop, bip bop bap,
It's the Class 3 teachers' rap.

'Join in with me, I'm Mr C,
Come along, let's have some fun,
In the shining, shining, hot, hot sun.'

Bip bop, bip bop bap,
It's the Class 3 teachers' rap.

Miss Barwise is really cool,
And she loves teaching at Gosforth School.
She likes to watch footie, supports Man U,
She loves Piglet and Winnie the Pooh.

Bip bop, bip bop bap,
It's the Class 3 teachers' rap.

Bip bop, bip bop bap,
It's the Class 3 teachers' rap.

Class 3
Gosforth CE Primary School

Trees In Season

Tree in spring
I can feel my branches once again
I see children all around me.
What's this? Buds on my branches
They're all coming back to me!

Tree in summer

Green busy leaves are all over my branches,
Children are playing on me, once again.
I feel like a new tree.

Tree in autumn.

I feel a teardrop falling down my trunk,
I just stand there watching my leaves desert me!
Only a couple of leaves are left on my branches,
I am all alone.

Tree in winter

Sparkling cobwebs hang from my branches,
I look like a Mr Whippy ice cream
With my trunk so bare and my top so white.
I am cold and naked.

Nicole Trainor (10)
Gosforth CE Primary School

Alone In the Home

Alone
Alone
Is the young little girl
Who lives in the children's home.

Sad
Sad
Is the little girl
She is never bad.

Silent
Silent
Is the young girl
She is never violent.

Old
Old
Is the battered house
It is full of dirt and mould.

They say she's a ghost,
That she came back to haunt the place
And that she keeps in her bedroom
A mysterious case
She never talks to anyone
And hates everything
That she sits in a dark room,
Waiting for the phone to ring.

I wonder
I wonder
As I lie in my bed
Does she have thoughts inside her head?
Is she really a ghost
Who likes to be all alone?
Or a sad little girl
Left in a home?

Hannah Skeen (10)
Gosforth CE Primary School

Winter

The snow is falling onto the ground,
Not one bit is making a sound.
The trees are bare,
The kids shout, 'Yeah!'
All the little kids go running around.

The rivers are crystal clear,
The fishes are swimming under the weir.
The snow is white
The clouds are near
The mums and dads have a lot of fear.

The wind is blowing here and there,
The snow is falling everywhere.
The holly berries are as red as red,
All the children are going to bed.

Charlotte Knowles (9)
Grayrigg CE Primary School

Trains

Faster than tractors, faster than cars
Faster than Pluto and faster than Mars
And see all the fields and the lakes
And I am eating a fat cake
Here is a farm, full of chickens
And I'm reading a book on Charles Dickens.

He is a person on the phone
Always using the same old tone
There is a car
And here is a Spar
All just whistling by
In the wink of an eye.

Robin Littlewood (11)
Grayrigg CE Primary School

Summer

The sun is shining onto the ground,
The birds are flying, round and round,
Looking for worms coming out of the ground.
The flowers are growing round and round.

The boys and girls are playing in the sun,
They're having lots of fun.
The trees are making not a sound
You can see them over the mound.

The school is closed
Mum and Dad have a doze,
Before the children are too excited to play.

Lucy Kelly (8)
Grayrigg CE Primary School

The Best Friends

There once was a girl called Miss Molly
She had a friend called Miss Polly
But they fell apart
So she went to the mart
To buy a new friend, in her trolley.

Josie Gledhill (10)
Grayrigg CE Primary School

Dragon

D astardly, dangerous dragon
R ampaging, raging dragon
A ngry, annoyed dragon
G rumpy, grouchy dragon
O utstanding, obstinate dragon
N aughty, nasty, natural dragon.

Joe Clement (8)
Grayrigg CE Primary School

Animals

A is for ants, running and scuttling
N is for newts who swim in ponds
I is for insects, pinching and scratching
M is for mice, eating cheese
A is for antelopes running around
L is for lambs, skipping and prancing
S is for seagulls flying about.

Henry Knowles (11)
Grayrigg CE Primary School

Animal

G is for giraffes which are spotted
I is for insects that crawl along
R is for red robin's breast
A is for anteaters, seldom seen
F is for flamingos, all pink and white
F is for the feathery leaves that giraffes eat
E is for elephants with long trunks.

Shahra Halstead (8)
Grayrigg CE Primary School

Winter

W is for winter all cold and wet
I is for icicles which drop down from rooftops
N is for the snow, nipping my nose
T is for tall trees, all bare and dull
E is for eating really hot food
R is for rain which comes down like a drizzle.

Stephen Park (10)
Grayrigg CE Primary School

What If?

What if trees had branches which hung
with sugar candy canes -
and golden sticky syrup falls when it rains?

Each house that you go into is
made of gingerbread.
Apart from the windows which
are smothered in chocolate spread?

What if the clouds are candyfloss pink,
white and blue -
and the sun is a big gobstopper that is
very hard to chew?

Hundreds and thousands hit the ground,
just like hailstones,
people run around and catch them in
their ice cream cones
children jump into their icing-covered bed,
they puff up their marshmallow pillows
for their head.

Bryoni Holland (9)
Grayrigg CE Primary School

Pirates

They work, they fight, they have many rests,
They break open all the treasure chests.
They punch, they kick, they fire and shoot,
If you have a fight, you'll get the boot.
Pirates smell horrid, they reek, they're rank,
If you're naughty you'll walk the plank.
They pull the sails up and don't care if they rip,
Are you scared?
You're aboard a pirate ship!

Oliver Philpott-Smith (10)
Grayrigg CE Primary School

Late

Walked out of the garden,
Gate clanged, 'Shut me!'
'Can't,' I said, 'late.'

Getting into the car
Birds whistled, 'Listen to our singing,'
'Can't!' I said. 'Late.'

Driving to work
Billboards shout, 'Slow down and read us.'
'Can't!' I said. 'Late.'

Get into work
Kettle whistles 'Grab a cuppa.'
'Can't!' I said. 'Late.'

Sit at my desk
Clock ticks, 'Look at me silly.'
'Oh no!' I said. 'I'm early.'

Cariss Instance   (10)
Greengate Junior School

Late

Walking down the road,
Fence called, 'Stop for a chat?'
'Can't!' I said. 'Late!'

Got to the road
Road shouted, 'Don't run on my face!'
'Can't!' I said. 'Late!'

Ran to the gate,
Gate yelled, 'Don't slam me!'
'Can't,' I said, 'late!'

Laura Reid   (10)
Greengate Junior School

Scarecrows

Scarecrows don't move in the light
But they dance and
prance in the night
Scarecrows like to play all night
Until the sun peeps out
They do their job all day
Then dance, prance and
Play until the next day.

Liam Flynn (11)
Greengate Junior School

Crazy Lion

The sea fearless lion,
Pouncing and rumbling.
He prances all night and day,
With his mighty jaw and powerful paws,
Hour upon hour, he roars.
The rumbling, tumbling stones,
As he roars, roars, roar,
The raging sea lion roars,
As he tumbles and rumbles.

Kirsty Bagshaw (10)
Greengate Junior School

My Family

I was born into a family of love and care,
When I need my parents, they're always there.
I kiss and hug them with great love and respect,
And I always try to do what my parents expect!

Though we love, we still do fight,
Through the morning and in the night.
We eventually make up for it the next day,
My family and me are really happy at play.

Rhys Studt (10)
Greengate Junior School

Snow Beast

He slides in the winter snow,
People never watch him go by,
He is never cold in the night,
He sleeps in the icy snow.

The flock disappears by night,
When winter goes, he goes,
Nobody knows where he goes,
He's not seen in spring, summer or autumn,
Just in winter.

Scott Reynolds (11)
Greengate Junior School

Baby Sister

Out of my mum's belly - with a winge and a yawn,
March 13th is when she was born.
When she came out, she had a cry,
She moved her lips and it sounded like, 'Hi!'
Her name is Holly and her favourite word is 'Daddy'
She gets fed by her mummy
She is nine months old
And is as good as gold!

Steven Dominik Coleman (11)
Greengate Junior School

Crazy Snake

The sea is a crazy snake
Black and slimy, he crawls along
The sand, all day with its scaly skin and
Its slippery body, hour upon hour
He hisses at the tumbling
Stones and smashing, smashing,
Smashing, smashing.
The slippery sea snake hisses.

Charlotte Benson (10)
Greengate Junior School

Snow

Snow runs down the old, old lane
As adults come out they say
it's a pain!
They walk down the path and
hear a crinkle, crinkle
As snow flies off the car
with a sprinkle, sprinkle.
The children come out with a
hip, hip hooray
They are so glad it has snowed today.

Kirsty Kneale (11)
Greengate Junior School

The Friendly Snowman

It was cold and dark on a frosty night
when the hills were white.
Then a snowman came along and sang
a friendly song.
The friendly snowman had a
great big shock because
It was nearly noon and he was melting.
It was cold and dark on a frosty night
when the hills were white.

Michael Turnbull (10)
Greengate Junior School

One Winter's Day

On the first winter's morning
A white, Christmas card day
A wedding cake piled up high.
Frost on the ground, crunch, crunch, crunch.
People laughing and joking in the cold breeze,
Snowmen and snow angels wherever we look.

Children come out to play,
Adults with hair, so white.
From defrosting windows
From the night.

Nicola Dunstan (11)
Greengate Junior School

Winter's Frost

A new season is here,
Icicles have frozen by night,
But turned to water by dawn,
Frozen grass turns crispy and white.

Snowmen appear on every lawn,
Snowball fights soon begin,
Then the golden sun rises
And everything melts away.
But winter will soon disappear
In front of your own eyes.

John Blain (11)
Greengate Junior School

A Recipe For Happiness

Bowl of happiness, for riding on my bike,
Jug of joy, for laughing with all my friends,
Packet of praise, for doing well with my teacher,
Cup of kindness, to keep my friendship flowing,
Spoon of surprise, for doing well in lessons,
Whisk of smiles, to keep me happy.

I will let my bowl of happiness ride on my bike,
I will let my jug of joy laugh with all my friends,
I will let my packet of praise do well with my teacher,
I will let my cup of kindness keep my friendship flowing,
I will let my spoon of surprise do well in lessons,
I will let my whisk of smiles keep me happy.

All baked together, makes my special happiness cake!

Thomas Davies (10)
Heversham St Peter's CE Primary School

Leaping Dolphins

Waves leaping like dolphins
above the blue and white sea.
Seagulls swooping through the air
squawking like mad.
Lonely?

Ocean spreading
over the soft sand
journeyed from a far-off land
or a sewer perhaps?

Softly lapping
over scuttling crabs.
Moving sideways,
right or left.
Confused?

Jack Graham (8)
Heversham St Peter's CE Primary School

The Storm

Creeping round, boiling up,
Getting ready to strike.
Rain comes down and lightning flashes
It's a really spooky sight!

Slates sliding off the houses,
People getting scared,
Birds swooping from side to side,
Children hugging teddy bears

Claws ripping plants and trees,
Gardens getting flattened
He's getting very angry now
And everything is battered

The winds are slowing down
Having got his prey
Withdrawing his eagle's claws
The storm gradually soars away.

Holly Robinson (9)
Heversham St Peter's CE Primary School

In The Sunlight

Dolphins jumping
In the sunlight
Seeing whales
Splash their tails
Into the water
Hearing the water
In a shell
I love the sea.

Leah Rushton (8)
Heversham St Peter's CE Primary School

Bonfire Night

Bonfire night is lots of fun
we always wait till it's bedtime for the sun
bonfires blowing right up high
fireworks zooming round the sky.

Red, blue, yellow and orange,
gold and purple, silver and green,
the prettiest colours to be seen.

Little men dancing in the flames
calling everybody names
like Flame and Firework and things like that
when they see a cat they say, 'Scat, scat, scat.'

Red, blue, yellow and orange,
gold and purple, silver and green,
the prettiest colours to be seen.

Everybody dancing round the flames
till it's time for bed
when we say goodnight
to the orange, green, yellow and red.

Red, blue, yellow and orange,
gold and purple, silver and green,
the prettiest colours to be seen.

Sophie Richards (7)
Heversham St Peter's CE Primary School

The Beach

Sandcastles like a huge fort
Sand, like crushed up crisps on your body.
Bumpy pebbles like hard snowballs,
The waves, as calm as a cat sleeping
And the holes in the ground
Like a dent in a can.
The sea as bubbly as bubbly cola.

Alex Child (8)
Heversham St Peter's CE Primary School

The Giant Mountain

It's big and bold
And really cold
Climbing up the rock face
At a slow pace.

Mum, my legs are tired
Can we go down now?
Well can you see the top?
We're nearly at the top.

Huff puff, never stop
Huff puff until the top.
Where's the view?
The mist guards it.
Nothing to see at the top.

Alex Hyman (7)
Heversham St Peter's CE Primary School

Teddies

My teddies keep me warm at night
When I am frightened
I hug them tight

Hug, hug, hug, hug
I hug them tight
Hug, hug, hug, hug
I hug them every night

When the monsters come out at night
And give me a fright
I hug my teddies really tight

Hug, hug, hug, hug
I hug them tight
Hug, hug, hug, hug
I hug them every night.

Robert McFadden (7)
Heversham St Peter's CE Primary School

Dogs

Dogs are beautiful
Dogs are cute
Just from puppies
Just too cute.

My dog's Sasha
Black and white
Small and hairy
Eyes beady, bright.

Dogs are beautiful
Dogs are cute
Just from puppies
Just too cute.

Sasha gets excited
When you rattle a tin
When she barks
She makes a din

Dogs are beautiful
Dogs are cute
Just from puppies
Just too cute.

Zak Crosby-McCann (7)
Heversham St Peter's CE Primary School

The Sea

The sea is
Lapping on my toes
Like a feather tickling me.

Dolphins diving
In the sun
Like a circus performing to me.

On the beach
On a sunny day.

Ben Robinson (7)
Heversham St Peter's CE Primary School

From The Upstairs Of A Double-Decker Bus

Street by street,
London's a treat
From the top of a bus.

The London Eye
Rotates on by
Like the world
In the sky.

Street by street,
London's a treat
From the top of a bus.

Buckingham Palace
With soldiers around
They might get tired
But they keep their ground.

Street by street,
London's a treat
From the top of a bus.

Big Ben is so tall
He makes me feel small
Every hour he'll always chime
Keeping Londoners on time.

Street by street,
London's a treat
From the top of a bus.

London is a wonderful place
Interesting things in every space
I see smiles on every face
What a lovely city for the human race!

Alice Pickthall (9)
Heversham St Peter's CE Primary School

Countryside

The countryside is a pretty place
Full of trees and flowers
It has its funny ways
And its special powers.

It has mountains, caves,
Cows and sheep,
And lots of juicy
Fruits to eat.

There's great old oak
And gentle birch,
In a strong wind
Their figures lurch.

If you go out on a cold day
You sometimes need a hat,
A long walk keeps you active
With friends you stop to chat.

I just like being outside
Surrounded by the countryside.

Eilish McDougall (9)
Heversham St Peter's CE Primary School

Energy Food

Pasta, pasta makes you run faster.
Pie, pie makes me jump high.
Peas, peas make you climb trees.
Beans, beans makes me roll in jeans.
Toast, toast makes me skip the most.

Emma Handley (8)
Heversham St Peter's CE Primary School

Mobile

My mobile is as small as a biscuit
I'm talking to my biscuit?
Oh crumbs!

Ring, ring, ring, tone,
Got to answer my phone.

My mobile calls my friends,
My mobile calls my mum,
Oh and my dad.

Ring, ring, ring, tone,
Got to answer my phone,

My mobile fits in my pocket
My mobile fits in my bag
Oh and in my hand.

Ring, ring, ring, tone,
Got to answer my phone.

Hello, oh it is you
Have you had a good day?
Oh I'm coming round soon.

Ring, ring, ring, tone,
What would I do without my phone?

Katie Dootson (7)
Heversham St Peter's CE Primary School

English Breakfasts

How I love my English breakfasts
How I adore my crispy, fried egg and creamy yolk
How I munch my hash browns with a luscious crunch
How I desire the crispy brown sausage
How I admire the orangey-red beans and yummy insides
How I am fond of my English breakfasts!

Jamie Dootson (10)
Heversham St Peter's CE Primary School

Friends

We are the best of friends
Emma and I,
We sit at the same table
In Class 3,
Mrs Sanders is our teacher
We like her.
At playtime we are together
Sometimes.
Amy, Rosie and Victoria
Also play sometimes,
At lunchtime we all play,
Eat and play again.
At home time we say goodbye,
Amy, Rosie, Victoria, Emma and I.

Sarah Garnett (7)
Heversham St Peter's CE Primary School

Aussie Outback

Scorching sand
Roasting and sweltering
You hear the crackling bush fire
Blazing orange sun
You're in 45° heat
The fire is glowing in the distance

Kookaburras laughing and flying away
Kangaroos bounding out into the outback
Red-hot fire turning the bushes into black ash
Bush fire is coming closer
        and closer
                and closer!

Rosanna Ely (8)
Heversham St Peter's CE Primary School

Britain Is An Island

Britain is an island
With water all around
London is the capital
Where you will hear lots of sounds.

Britain is an island
With cities and towns
Bustling and busy
With people all around.

Britain is an island
With daffodils and heather
The rivers on the hillside
And lots of funny weather.

Sophie Fishwick (10)
Heversham St Peter's CE Primary School

The Dragon

A dragon came to the house
I was frightened
I crept downstairs
Dragon,
Dragon,
Dragon,
Dragon!
I ran upstairs
I told
Mum and Dad.
'Forget it,' they said.
I told Thomas my brother
He screamed!

Kimberley Nelson (7)
Heversham St Peter's CE Primary School

The Witches' Spell

Double, double toil and bubble
Fire cooled and cauldron trouble
Wool of fish, eye of adder
Lizard's head and seal's bladder
Tongue of dog and drunken man's swing
Baboon's butt and howlet's wing
For a charm of powerful trouble
Like a hell-broth boil and bubble.

Shell of cockroach, antennae of ant
Ear of bear, lizard's prance
Eye of flower, chopped tadpole's tail
Nuclear weapon and hurricane's hail
Old woman's stride, dreamer's dream
Stem of olive, silver screen
For a charm of powerful trouble
Like a hell-broth boil and bubble.

Jack Kerr (9)
Heversham St Peter's CE Primary School

Skipping Rhyme

One, one, having some fun
Two, two, make a shoe
Three, three, twist a key
Four, four, open the door
Five, five, I hate Clive
Six, six, pick up sticks
Seven, seven, go to Heaven
Eight, eight, it's getting late
Nine, nine, it's fine
Ten, ten, where is my hen?

Natasha Wightman (8)
Heversham St Peter's CE Primary School

Recipe For Happiness

To make my happy cake I need
special ingredients.
A packet of praise from my teacher
makes me glow inside.
A jug of pets to play with
makes me feel content.
A hug from Mummy when I do well
makes me feel good.
Friends to play with in the playground
makes me feel joyful.

I bring in the whisk
whirl and twirl the mixture.
I put it in the oven to bake together
then I serve it up to complete my
recipe for happiness.

Samuel Willacy (10)
Heversham St Peter's CE Primary School

My Recipe For Happiness

A packet of praise to make me feel positive,
A jug of friends to make me feel contented,
A cup of laughter to share with my best friends,
A spoonful of joy when riding my bike.
Then add a whisk to stir it around,
Then put it in the oven and watch it rise,
Then take it out and what do you have?
A happy, joyful and positive cake.
Then put it on some plates and if you eat it
You will be happy, joyful and positive.

William McFadden (10)
Heversham St Peter's CE Primary School

The Storm

Slates sliding off the roof
Pattering like a giant hoof

The wind went on tugging at a tree
I'm really glad it wasn't me!

Finally the vicious wind won
The life in the trees was nearly gone

Arms waving helplessly in the air
It really, really isn't fair!

Amy Fox (8)
Heversham St Peter's CE Primary School

Winter Morning

The snow was falling
Very early in the morning.

The children looked out of their windows
The cold north wind blows.

Snowball fights so big
Large trenches they had to dig.

Snowmen make a perfect target
As their mum went off to market.

Mum made vegetable soup
Just after loop-the-loop.

All the children took off their clothes
Soon after, they were warming up their toes.

Daniel Butterworth (8)
High Hesket Primary School

The Winter Day

Children playing down the street
Jumping with their frozen feet.
Down big snowballs fall
As you are throwing snowballs.
I need to sit by the fire to get some heat
While eating some meat.
Girls and boys on the ice
Skating is very, very nice.
Outside it is really cold
As I and other people rolled.
I have a very cold face
While I tie my shoelace.
Wearing winter clothes
When doing dancing shows.
Take a bit of cake
When ice skating on the lake.
Snowmen on the rooftops
Just the same as your tooth tops.
It is swirling down when it is snowing
Outside people are going.
I like the snow
When it is down low.
From my bed I am coming down
In my dressing gown.
Kids have snowball fights
All through the night.
Friends playing with each other
Without their mothers.
Big blobs of white snow gleams
As there are icy streams.

Megan Norwood (8)
High Hesket Primary School

Frozen Life

Snowmen getting built,
Then taken into the house wrapped in quilt.

Children sledging oh what fun!
Then Mum makes a crispy bun.

Frozen ponds covered in ice
To go skating would be nice.

Children throwing snowballs really hard
At the wall in the yard.

Snow is floating in the air
Poor old trees they are looking bare.

Dawn Gibson (8)
High Hesket Primary School

Snow

Snow is falling all around,
bits of snow falling on the ground.

The children play in crisp, white snow,
big round snowballs they like to throw.

The sky is like a blur,
when the children are wrapped in fur.

We go sledging,
while my mum is potato wedging.

I have been to dinner which was so nice,
instead of skating on the black ice.

Connie Wainwright (9)
High Hesket Primary School

A Frozen Snowman

A teaspoon of icy frost
4 dessert spoons of frosty white snow
A ladle of icy icicles
2 cups of magic frost leaves
1 bowl of white slush
3 buckets full of glittery trees
1 round of shimmering snowball
and all these things make a frozen
snowman.

Laura Atkinson (8)
High Hesket Primary School

Winter Day

The winter snowflakes falling down
When I get my cold crown.

Every snowflake falling cold
Many snowballs all ready and rolled.

All the icicles hanging cold
Of which I would not like to hold.

All the snow is so white
Looking so very bright.

Victoria Armstrong (9)
High Hesket Primary School

Winter Morning

Winter morning isn't boring
Waking up on a sparkly morning.

Fluffy snow I'd like to hold
Look at me I'm freezing cold.

Little snowflakes trickle down to the ground
Can you hear it make a sound?

Jade Robley (8)
High Hesket Primary School

The Winter World

The air lays down a blanket of snow
The children make footprints as they go
To make big snowmen in the white
It takes all morning and all night

And it is so very nice
To go ice skating in the ice.
We were sledging with our friends
Going straight and round the bends.

That's the place where it's nice to be
In the land of the frozen tree
Now it's spring and it is time
To roll up your blanket but you'll be fine.

But do not cry, do not fear
Winter will always come next year.
Wait in the sun, wait in the rain
Winter will always come again.

Matthew Usher (8)
High Hesket Primary School

A Winter Morning Recipe For A Snowman

A teaspoon of icy frost
2 dessert spoons of white snow
A tablespoon of rainy icicles
And three bowls of winter slush too.
A ladle of frozen trees
4 buckets of white snowmen.
5 cups of footprints
And a truck of frozen stones.

Put all of these together
And you'll get a perfect snowman.

Jamie Foster (8)
High Hesket Primary School

Winter's Day

Frozen children in the town
Nobody's going to the down.

Everyone's saying, 'It's so cold,
If we go out we'll be big and bold.'

Let's creep out to see the snow
Nobody else will want to go.

Come let's go out it will be fun
Then we'll go in for a hot currant bun.

Tabitha Clark (7)
High Hesket Primary School

Recipe For Winter

A teaspoon of hard ice
A dessert spoon of cold mountains
Two tablespoons of freezing cold snow
A cupful of snowballs
Three bowls of frozen lakes
A ladle of white frost
A bucket of flying snowflakes
That's what makes winter.

Josh Brown (8)
High Hesket Primary School

A Recipe For A Blizzard

Two dessert spoons of frozen leaves that are cold and icy
A tablespoon of soft snow
One tornado, strong and windy
A bucket of icicles, spiky and hard
One snow boulder really fat and snowy
Mix it all together and you get a blizzard.

Joshua Noble (9)
High Hesket Primary School

Winter

Children have snowball fights
As I put away my kites.

I walk through the white snow
Leaving footprints in the snow.

Oh no, big round snowballs
They like to throw.

The temperature is dropping it is minus ten,
So I brought a blanket and made a den.

Children make snowmen on the fell,
After snowmen watch the children ring the big bell.

When it is gone it is very sad,
Making people go so mad.

Lucy Thomson (9)
High Hesket Primary School

The Snowfall

Take a bite
because it's all white
and it's alright.

I like the snow,
when it's in a bow,
I love the snow
when it is low.

Snow on the rooftops
just like tooth tops.

Arran Johnston (8)
High Hesket Primary School

Winter Day

I wear my old clothes
when it snows.

School is closed
because it snowed.

Snowflakes are dancing all around
children are throwing snowballs as big as a pound.

There are lots of sparkling icicles
on our bicycles.

Amy Ellams (8)
High Hesket Primary School

Falling Snow

The snow is falling all around
It makes a trickly sound.
So cold I walk through snow
Where it comes from I'd like to know.
The snow makes children cold
Lying down they are rolled.
It makes a blanket over the world
Lying by the fire I'm much warmer when I'm curled.

Hannah Butterworth (7)
High Hesket Primary School

All About Winter

White snow fell down
Now winter is no frown.

The snowflakes fluttered to the ground
Children twirling round and round.

The trees are dying
But birds are still flying.

Hannah Barthel (8)
High Hesket Primary School

A Recipe For A Snowy Day

A bowl of giant snowballs
A dessert spoon of sledges
With reindeer
A giant oven full of children
A ladle of frozen leaves
Two cupfuls of ice
With frozen leaves on top
A kettle full of frozen trees
A bucketful of snow and frost.

Put all these things together
To make a snowy day.

Joseph Dixon (8)
High Hesket Primary School

Snow

Fluffy, furry snow
The poor children can't wear a bow.

The snow is cool
The children go to the pool
But not to school.

The snow is mushy
And very slushy.

Emily Sant (7)
High Hesket Primary School

A Winter Cake

Two teaspoons of frost
Half a teaspoon of sledges
Three cups of cocoa
Nine bowls of wellies
Two ladles of gloves
And a bucket of numb toes.

Henry Wainwright (7)
High Hesket Primary School

Cold Morning

The world looks so round
Children playing, lots of snow being found.
Big, cold snowflakes falling on the rooftops
As well as the ground.
The children throwing snowballs at the ground
With some sound.
Snowmen being built, marks of snowballs on the front.
With one big shunt
Down he goes with a grunt.
I go up to my bedroom and under the quilt, I wait until dawn.
Morning has come, the first place to look is the lawn.
I wobble out of bed
And go downstairs to get fed.

Jonathan Turnbull (7)
High Hesket Primary School

A Snowy Morning Recipe

A teaspoon of clouds
A dessertspoon of icy icicles
A cup of frost
6 bowls of wind
A ladle of sledges
8 buckets of snow.

Robbie Sisson (8)
High Hesket Primary School

Winter Recipe

A teaspoon of ice
A dessertspoon of snow
A bucket of frost
3 and a half bowls of snowballs
A cup of water
A ladle of snowmen.

Danny Ewin (7)
High Hesket Primary School

Winter

Winter, winter, icy cold,
Everyone is so cold, their face is bold.

Winter, winter, frosty trees,
Lots of children have icy knees.

Winter, winter, frozen ground,
The world is so cold it can hardly turn around.

Katie Butterworth (7)
High Hesket Primary School

Winter Wonderland

I like to target the wall with snow
The snow I think is like dough

I hide down in the den
When the snow pecks me like a hen

From the frozen nests of geese
Eggs roll at me like a beast.

Thomas Perfect (8)
High Hesket Primary School

The Haunted House

As the screaming zombie walks through the dark night
Three ugly witches give people terrifying frights.
As for the ghost, he's funny and gleaming
Because loads of people run away screaming.
So now I have warned you, you'll probably shout
Once you go in there you'll never get out!

Christian Sloan (7)
Holy Family Catholic School

Silky The Otter

I know a little otter
It has a brown coat
It lives at the aquarium next to the boat.

It lives with its big friends
It likes to play a game
Its favourite food is fish
And Silky is its name.

Amy Pryer (7)
Holy Family Catholic School

As High As A Cloud

As high as a cloud
As high as a plane
As high as a star
As high as a bird
As high as a rocket
As high as a jet
As high as a balloon.

Patrick Allington (7)
Holy Family Catholic School

Shark

There is a gigantic shark
Who's hungry for his tea
One thing I do hope is
That he doesn't eat me!
He's very mean
And he's getting very hungry
Although I think he's smiling
And he's invited me for tea.

Philip McArthur (7)
Holy Family Catholic School

The Haunted House

The *haunted house*
is such a fright.
The *haunted house*
is always dark at night.
The *haunted house*
a horrible sight.
The *haunted house*
is an awful scare.
The *haunted house*
was in my nightmare.
So now I have warned you
please beware.
Whoever goes in there
will never get out!

Jane Gerrard (7)
Holy Family Catholic School

Season Haikus

Spring
Jumping lambs in fields
Birds sing happily in spring
Flowers start to sprout.

Summer
I like to sunbathe
In the summer holidays
On a soft deckchair.

Autumn
The golden leaves fall
While the wind blows others down
To land on soft ground.

Winter
All the leaves have gone
Bye autumn, hello winter
Snow begins to fall.

Christopher Littlechild (9)
Ireleth St Peter's Primary School

November 5th

And you big rocket,
I see how wildly you fly,
Shooting up and zooming by,
Exploding in the midnight air
And falling down without a care.

Catherine wheel
I see how happily you spin,
Zooming round upon your pin,
Cleaning the air with beautiful flames,
In the lush green park where the children play games.

Roman candle
You explode, touching the glowing moon,
I know that you will come down soon,
Sparkling up and falling down
And shining like a sparkling crown.

And so
It's the end of the night,
There's nothing left in sight.
Down go the ashes,
As everybody dashes.

Ellysia Wallace (9)
Ireleth St Peter's Primary School

Storm

One evening in the middle of a ruthless storm,
I awoke to see a gory battlefield outside,
A deafening roar echoed around town.
Heavy rainfall, impersonating Niagara Falls,
Lightning was a searchlight,
Lighting up the midnight sky,
Animals ran for shelter,
Like evacuees escaping the war zone.

Carl Hall (11)
Ireleth St Peter's Primary School

Beach

One morning I woke to see the sun shining bright,
Turning the beach into Heaven.
Sun, sea and sand mixed together,
Which I found hard to resist,
Like not resisting your favourite toy.
I ran down to the beach,
Like a bolt of lightning.
The moment my feet stepped onto the sand,
They felt warm.
The calm blue waves splashed over the sand,
Making it silky and wet.
My feet dug deep
In the warm, fast sinking sand,
The sun burnt my back.
It was a perfect place.
The waves overlapped again
Like a touch of warmth and happiness.

Leanne Bevan (10)
Ireleth St Peter's Primary School

Garden

The garden was like Heaven,
A sweet scent like perfume covered the air,
Roses like a heart in the corner,
The tulips are blue as the bluest sky,
A stream of glittering water crossed through the garden like a snake,
Birds cheeping like a harp,
A vine swing covered in blossom,
I gazed around the garden under the old oak tree,
Eating my picnic,
The sunshine made me sleepy.

Jamie Tyson (10)
Ireleth St Peter's Primary School

Snow

One morning, outside my window was a winter wonderland!
It was like a white blanket enveloping the Earth.
I decided to explore this huge place
So I slipped on my hat and boots and ran through the door,
Like a lightning bolt.
I can remember now, the tornado.
Wind circled round our street
Icy lake like a frozen man's face,
Leafless trees were a person's bony fingers.
Icicles shimmered and glimmered on the rooftops,
Children were everywhere, ice-skating, snowball fighting,
Snowman making and making angel prints in the snow.
The sun came from behind the clouds
And made everything glitter like sequins.

Melissa Kirkby (10)
Ireleth St Peter's Primary School

The Battlefield

One stormy night, the rain was falling from Heaven.
The rain was like someone crying.
Then a bolt of thunder, like a lion in distress, roared
Its loud noise as though it was pleading for life
As though the sky was in agony,
Crying for help. Then a quick flash of lightning,
Like an ostrich running at top speed.
It was like a battlefield. I started to look at the sky.
It was beautiful, colours of white, yellow,
Blue, pink, red, black, orange, silver,
And gold with a hint of green.
I covered my ears, the noise deafening
Me as I stood in the battlefield.

Daniel Tyson (11)
Ireleth St Peter's Primary School

Sunset

The sunset is like
Wonderful pieces of gold,
Beneath clear waters,
Shining softly.

The red sky is a flame of beauty
Shining sweetly on pearls,
Leaving the sky.

Can't every sunset be as perfect?
The sun is over the hill,
Ready to hibernate
From the sky once more.

Shimmers of the water,
A repeat of fiery skies,
Like a golden cloak,
Covering the sky,
Over the world.

Kate Whittle (11)
Ireleth St Peter's Primary School

Terrible Devastation

Dreadful thoughts running through my mind,
I feel as if nobody is being kind,
Deadly bombs approaching us by night,
I feel I might be in for a *fright*,
I look on to the terrible mess,
Which lies upon the city Inverness.

Sitting in the air raid shelter,
The bombs dropping helter skelter,
The horrific sounds,
Losing our pounds,
Drinking my pop, just thinking this would *stop!*

Catherine Steele (10)
Ireleth St Peter's Primary School

Storm

A storm struck,
I pulled my hood close to my ears,
Rain began to pour, smashing on the roof,
Like boulders in an avalanche.
Lighting flashed furiously lighting up the sky,
With fireworks and jumping jacks, lively golden rain,
Which fell jerkily to the ground.
A gust of wind flew past, turning over cars,
That went flying loudly into a topsy-turvy world.

Sam Broadley (11)
Ireleth St Peter's Primary School

Rebecca Hill

I heard nothing
But horses galloping in grassy fields,
Where flowers grew like a colourful army
In a forest of grass.
Fluffy white lambs dotted the landscape
Like flecks of snow,
Like a star gleaming in the distance.
I saw the sea flashing silver beams,
Wrapped in a sequinned gown.

Rosie Whittle (11)
Ireleth St Peter's Primary School

Doves

The doves that are white like snow,
Glisten, blinding your eyes,
The children watch the doves till the sun dies down,
But the doves stay there like they are frozen to the moon,
When the sun comes back the doves play,
And come down to the spongy grass to nibble on their feast.

Ruth Fitzsimmons (10)
Ireleth St Peter's Primary School

November The Fifth

And you big rocket,
I see your colourful sparks,
As you zoom quickly over the parks,
With your thin tail trailing,
You look like you're sailing.

Catherine wheel
As we watch you spin through the air,
Lovely colours do not scare,
I watch your colours go round and round,
I love listening to your sound.

Roman candle
I see your flame rise higher and higher,
Opening up your ball of fire,
Falling to the ground,
Squealing like a hound.

And so,
Now the bonfire has been done,
No more fireworks, no more fun,
Now everyone will remember,
The fifth of November.

Emily Burns (9)
Ireleth St Peter's Primary School

Spring Haiku

Birds build nests in trees,
Daffodils and flowers grow,
The middle of spring.

Guy Belsey (9)
Ireleth St Peter's Primary School

The Magical River

I sat amidst the trees with my picnic,
The birds' special song surrounded me with contentment.
Sweet, magical music filled my ears,
As the river trickled
Like a glass waterfall
Beneath the rippling water.
Gold and silver fish dart,
Happily - like a shooting star,
Other fish scatter past, as
Frogs bounce playfully.

Rebekah Walker (11) & Kathryn Knipe (10)
Ireleth St Peter's Primary School

What Is Green?

What is green? A snake is green
slithering through the jungle scene.

What is black? A rat is black
crawling through the sewage sack.

What is red? A tiger's jaw is red
eating a deer's head.

What is grey? A rabbit is grey
hopping on a sunny day.

What is blue? A shark is blue
eating all the fishes too.

What is white? A swan is white
sailing in the daylight.

Geordie Smith (8)
Jericho Primary School

The Jungle

The jungle is calm, the jungle is dark,
The wolves are howling and dogs bark,
Nobody is there, not even a hare,
In the jungle nobody's fair.

The jungle is scary,
There are lots of things that are hairy,
The gorillas are dancing,
The monkeys are prancing,
In the jungle nobody is fair.

The jungle is quiet,
But the animals can start a riot,
Alligators are swimming,
Monkeys are swinging,
In the jungle nobody is fair.

Matthew Johnson (9)
Jericho Primary School

The Cheetah

The cheetah strolling round
Looking for its prey.
Hiding in the long green grass.
Creeping closer getting ready!
The yellow vicious eyes,
Looking at its big fat prey.
I metre between them.

Run! Run! Run! The cheetah running faster!
No way out for the prey now.
Pounce!
Surely he's got it - yes he has!

Connor Miller (9)
Jericho Primary School

Cool Cars

C is for car
O is for oil
O is for oxygen
L is for lap of the race track

C is for cool
A is for Audi
R is for rally car
S is for Subaru speeding in the light.

Michael Lythgoe (8)
Jericho Primary School

Football

F is for the foot that kicks the ball
O is for the officials that watch the match
O is for the players offside
T is for the teams that play
B is for the ball whizzing around the pitch
A is for Aston Villa my favourite team
L is for Leeds on the last leg
L is for let's play football!

Josh McDonald (9)
Jericho Primary School

School Days

S chool gates open
C hildren charge in
H olidays are far away
O n the whiteboard the teacher writes
O ver and over the children copy in their books
L oud and welcome the school bell rings.

Eleanor M Midwood (8)
Jericho Primary School

School Poetry

Who is shy? Scarlett is shy,
especially when she starts to cry.

Who is smart? Steve is smart,
especially when it comes to art.

Who is sweet? Samantha is sweet,
especially when she starts to eat.

Who is good? George is good,
especially when he avoids the mud.

Who is mad? Merlin is mad,
especially when he is very bad.

Aaron Wynd (9)
Jericho Primary School

Anita

Anita annoyed the teacher,
She didn't know what to do,
She found out straight away,
Why she came down this road,
She had put a frog in teacher's water,
She had torn up all the fairytales,
Had written on the wall,
Anita got detention. She wasn't happy at all.
Her parents came to see the teacher,
Anita ran up the wall.

Jessica Longrigg (8)
Jericho Primary School

What Is Brown?

What is brown? A monkey's brown
wearing a fluffy crown.

What is red? A python's red
sleeping in a jungle bed.

What is yellow? A canary's yellow
squeaking his loudest bellow.

What is green? Why, a frog is green
being lean and mean.

What is black? A bat is black
hiding in a dusty sack.

Louise Banks (8)
Jericho Primary School

School Poetry

S is for shoes that boys wear,
C is for cake that boys eat,
H is for happy boys,
O is for outside, outside the school where the boys play,
O is for the outstanding school where the boys play,
L is for lunch when the boys eat,

B is for boys that play together,
O is for oranges that boys eat,
Y is for the new year when school starts,
S is for school.

Joshua Benson (8)
Jericho Primary School

I'm Getting A New Pet

I'm getting a pet. I'm getting a mouse.
But Mum said it would scamper around the house.

I'm getting a pet. I'm getting two cats.
I have chosen two. But Dad said I couldn't have them
because they eat rats.

I'm getting a pet. I'm getting a dog.
But then I changed my mind - I'm getting
A frog!

Charlotte Louise Wilson (8)
Jericho Primary School

What Is Gold?

What is gold? A bear is gold
like the sun so bright.

What is grey? Squirrels are grey
like the morning light.

What is blue? A kingfisher is blue
like the midday sky.

What is black? A blackbird is black
like the midnight sky.

Rachel McKenna (8)
Jericho Primary School

What Is Pink?

What is pink? A rose is pink
When people blink.

What is blue? Fruit is blue,
When you say phooo!

What is black? The sky is black,
When it gets the sack.

Andrew Bennett (9)
Jericho Primary School

The Girl Lost In Sea

The sea seething
the girl breathing
little girl screaming

Wind beaming
parents depressed
they need a rest
the sea getting rougher
little girl getting tougher

Up, up the water is rising upon the boat
everything is beginning to float
she wrote on her arm
she will never forget her loving family
the boat sank softly with the girl in
bye bye.

Georgia Batty (9)
Jericho Primary School

What Is White?

What is white? The snow is white,
Falling in the winter's light.

What is wet? The rain is wet,
Dropping round you like a net.

What is cold? The wind is cold,
Whistling and whirling when it gets a hold.

What is yellow? The sun is yellow,
Shining down bright and mellow.

Bethany Guy (8)
Jericho Primary School

If I Was A Dog

If I was a dog
I would never eat a frog
If I was a cat
I would never sleep in a hat

If I was a mouse
I wouldn't live in a house
If I was a snake
I would never eat steak

If I was a frog
I would live in a bog
But if I was me
I would be as happy as can be.

Jemma Tegg (9)
Jericho Primary School

What Is Yellow?

What is yellow? The sun is yellow
shining and bright.

What is brown? A monkey is brown
eating all the bananas.

What is red? A rose is red
standing in the field.

What is green? The grass is green
in the summer light.

Evie Long (8)
Jericho Primary School

If I Was A Bird

If I was a bird I would live in a nest,
But if I was a monkey I would scratch my chest.

If I was a rabbit I would eat lots of carrots,
If I was an eagle I would chirp like parrots.

If I was a frog I would live in a bog,
But if I was a dog I would run like a hog.

But it's not very fair because I am only human.

Josh Shepherd (8)
Jericho Primary School

My Life

I have an annoying sister, she is very young,
She's like a baby rhino always pratting about,
She likes annoying me, which I don't, she is like a stubborn tongue,
I really want to kill her, bit I just can't, and this is my life.

I have an older brother, he is very old,
He's like a father rhino always bossing you about,
He likes bossing me around, which I don't, he's like a stubborn cold,
I really want to kill him, but I just can't, and this is my life.

Matthew Brown (8)
Jericho Primary School

My Horse

My horse is so cute
He loves to eat
He loves sugar-free Polos
And when I put him out
He's always rolling about
He's always mucky
So I decided to bring him in
And make a start on grooming him.

Paige Carson (8)
Jericho Primary School

Fast Racing

F ast and furious,
A nd cool but useless
S tarting in their lanes
T urning on the throttle.

R ipped body shells,
A ppetite for driving lower and lower,
C ars crashing,
I nto the pits,
N o getting out,
G ood ending - people starting to shout.

Mitchell Rogan (9)
Jericho Primary School

What Is It?

It's funny,
It's weak,
It's just been born!

It's dancing,
It's jumping,
It's lively and young!

It's flapping,
It's flying,
It's testing its wings!

Now it's heading south for winter!

Kieran Scotchbrook (9)
Jericho Primary School

Birds Of A Feather

Birds of a feather,
All swooping together,
Are such a lovely sight,
In the soothing twilight.

And as I go to bed,
Thoughts running through my head,
Remind me of the sight,
I saw that summer's night.

Libby Gibson (10)
Levens CE School

Middle Pages

If you can't judge a book by its cover,
And you can only judge a person by their soul,
Then how do we find these middle pages or heart?
Do we sit and wait for them to unfold,
Or do we need to look deeper,
Maybe even to the back of the book,
Or maybe,
Just maybe, do we really need to look?

Milly Hammond (10)
Levens CE School

Snakes

Snakes slither and slide all day long,
'Nothing can go wrong'
They're right and right they are.
They dream of travelling afar,
To a distant land,
No one needs to give them a hand.
Snakes slither and slide all day long.
'Nothing can go wrong.'

Elliot Morrow (9)
Newbarns Primary School

Sweets

Sweets, sweets
Lovely sweets

Cola bottles, jelly beans,
All chewy and sweet.

Sour sweets burn my mouth,
Like the fire on a fire ball.

Lollipops take forever to eat,
Candy sticks all powdery and white.

Marshmallows soft, squidgy and light,
Flying saucers fizzy and nice.

But chocolate is my favourite,
It's milky and creamy as it melts in my mouth.

Yummy, yummy, yummy.

Daniel Sheppard (9)
Newbarns Primary School

Football, Football

Football, football is my game
Golf and rugby just aren't the same.
Running around with all my friends
I hope the fun will never end.

The whistle blows to start the match
I run down the field and make a pass.
Dribbling, tackling, kicking the ball
If we do our best, we can beat them all.

The greatest feeling in the world
Is when you score the winning goal
Football, football is the best
It's so much better than the rest.

Christian Roberts (8)
Newbarns Primary School

When I Play My PlayStation

When I play my PlayStation
It feels just like I'm there
I can ride a skateboard
Flying through thin air.

When I play my PlayStation
I can go back to the past
Chasing after dinosaurs
The raptors run real fast.

When I play my PlayStation
I can swing like Spider-Man
Climbing up the skyscrapers
Catch me if you can.

When I play my PlayStation
Doing magic tricks
Me and Harry Potter
There is nothing we can't fix.

When I play my PlayStation
Time goes by so fast
Dad says you've been on it an hour
Make that game your last.

Jonathan Atkinson (8)
Newbarns Primary School

The Player

Roll up, roll up
Come and watch the game
Of the player with a perfect aim
Michael Owen is his name

Liverpool is his team
Scoring goals is routine
For this player so supreme.

Sophie Fisher (9)
Newbarns Primary School

I'm Moving House Today!

I'm moving to a new house today
hip hip hooray!
Here come the removal men
John, Paul and Ben.
They park their lorry
to load all our things
And tie up the boxes
with pieces of string.

We say goodbye
as we shut the door
And pick up the last
few things off the floor.
I can't wait to see my new house
all sunny and bright.
And sleep in my new
bedroom later on tonight.

Scott J McKenna (9)
Newbarns Primary School

The Rocket

At the bottom of the garden the bonfire is burning bright,
Here comes the first rocket,
Bang!
Wow! Now it's out of sight,
Here comes the next one flying high,
Now it's faded in the sky.

We are toasting marshmallows pink and white,
We've set the sparklers all alight.

All ten of us are in a row, watching our fireworks go,
The bonfire is dying low and red,
I think it's time to go to bed.

Eve Mulholland (8)
Newbarns Primary School

My Little Brother

I have a little brother
He's only eight months old
We cuddle him and keep him warm
So he's never cold.

My little brother
Has big blue eyes
He looks like my mother
And hardly ever cries.

He has the softest baby hair
And the cutest little smile
He cuddles his teddy bear
We are always there
We always care.

Holly Cooksey (8)
Newbarns Primary School

My Holiday

I can't wait to go on holiday,
I booked it last week.
I've got my suitcase ready,
and I'm folding my clothes very neat.

I am going with all my family,
my smelly brother too,
I hope we don't forget him,
lest he will have to stay at the zoo!

My rabbit is staying with my nana,
but she doesn't know what to do.
I can't wait to go on holiday,
Mum, can't you?

Jessie Wilson (8)
Newbarns Primary School

Down By The Beach

I love to go down to the beach
and play in all the pools,
We have a game of volleyball
but usually I lose.

The pools are full of little fish
I catch them with my net,
They squirm and wriggle all around
and I get really wet!

Many children play in the sand.
they seem to have such fun.
They build their castles all day long
by the light of the warming sun.

Soon it is time for the children to go
they're as tired as can be,
The only thing we can hear now
is the sound of the lapping sea.

Samuel Benson (9)
Newbarns Primary School

The Christmas Gift

What I got for Christmas
Was no ordinary toy,
You won't find it at a home,
Of any other girl or boy.

What I got for Christmas,
Wasn't a teddy or a train,
I didn't get a doll house,
What I got certainly wasn't plain.

What I got was the real one,
The real one and only,
What I got was the key to the door of the world,
All long and thin and bony.

Eleanor Ogilvie (9)
Newbarns Primary School

The World Of Birds And Wings

As the bluebird flies up in the sky
And the owls sit in their holes,
The seagull soars above the sea
And dives down to greet his friends and family
And the eagle swoops down to catch his prey
And the parrots fly above the trees
As I sit at home and play with my budgie
All we can wonder about is the
World of birds and wings.

Eve Buzzocott (9)
Newbarns Primary School

Missing PlayStation

I had a PlayStation once
I woke up one day and it was gone
Where it went I don't know
Father Christmas knows that I grow

It was a night of snow
When he came I do not know
Thankfully he brought me something new
My PlayStation 2 meant that I was no longer blue.

Daniel Johnston (8)
Newbarns Primary School

My Birthday

O n your birthday the 3rd of Feb
L oads of love from Nanna is sent.
I n my eyes you are one special kid,
V ote you the top of every list.
E specially good looking, a real cool dude.
R eady smile, lifts everyone's mood.

Oliver Chapman (9)
Newbarns Primary School

In The Jungle

Here in the jungle,
as quiet as night,
I saw a tiger
it gave me a fright.

A lion roared
as it went by,
it made me wish
that I could fly.

Snakes and spiders
in the wet,
leave me feeling
numb with sweat.

In the jungle
and up in the hill
beasts are searching
for the kill.

They follow me here
they follow me there,
I'm glad I didn't
meet up with a bear.

Daniel Hall (9)
Newbarns Primary School

Ooey Gooey

Ooey gooey was a sweet
A sticky sweet it was,
It stuck upon the sole of my shoe
And never did it come off.

Ooey gooey!

Zoe Byers (8)
Newbarns Primary School

White Fluffy Snow

I wish it would snow
all fluffy and white
as soft as cotton wool
from day until night.

Throwing snowballs is such fun
make it big
throw it quick
and run, run, run.

Build a snowman as high as can be
with eyes, nose and mouth
a hat and a scarf
I'm freezing cold now
and ready for a warm cup of tea.

Tom Purdy (9)
Newbarns Primary School

Summer Days

Summer days when the sun is hot
We like to play with water a lot.
We splish and splash, squirt and laugh,
It's the only time we like a bath.

Summer days are a real scream,
We paddle at the beach and eat ice cream.

Summer holidays are much more fun,
No school to attend or homework to be done.

We lie on our backs and look at the sky
Listening to the birds go by.

Samuel Wilkes (9)
Newbarns Primary School

The Chocolate World

I was in bed snoring,
Snoring my head away,
When I had a nightmare,
I woke up and cried.

My mum came up and said,
'Don't cry! Think of good thing!'
So I went back to bed.

Then I woke up suddenly,
I went into another world,
Full of chocolate people,
Trees and everything.

I had the coolest time,
Then I found out it was a dream!

Roxanne White (9)
Newbarns Primary School

Chocolate Cake

I love chocolate cake,
I really love the taste,
The only trouble is . . .
It adds inches to my waist.

Melissa Hogan (8)
Newbarns Primary School

Winter

The winter freezes all the ponds
The winter is very cold
In the winter you can build a snowman
So children can have fun
Winter fills all the ground
With beautiful snow all around.

Rebecca Athersmith (7)
Our Lady of the Rosary RC Primary School

When I Grow Up!

When I grow up I'm going to be an astronaut, a pilot or a
                                        helicopter flier,
I'm going to be a vet, a dog carer or an owner of a cattery.

When I grow up I'm going to be a jester, a juggler or a funny clown,
I'm going to be a sweet shop owner, work at Tesco or the Co-op.

When I grow up I'm going to be a doctor, a nurse or an
                                        ambulance driver,
I'm going to be a teacher, headmistress or a helper at a school.

When I grow up I'm going to be a barmaid, a waitress or own a pub,
I'm going to be a priest, a vicar or help at the church.

When I grow up I'm going to be a professional piano player
                                        and good at recorder
I'm going to be a judge in the government or even a queen.

I just can't decide what to be.

Bethany Thomason (8)
Our Lady of the Rosary RC Primary School

Winter Spring

Winter drifts through the night
Making snowflakes in my sight
Throwing snowballs in the air
With a little glare

Spring - back to bed in the morning
Flowers glow, red blue and yellow
Sun glowing all around
Can't believe it! What a sound!

Rebecca Jane Smith (7)
Our Lady of the Rosary RC Primary School

On The School Playground

Children playing tig
Children doing the jig
Little children putting on a wig
Some children are really big

Swings and red slides
Grass and green vines
Children sitting on the sides
Children doing hard lines.

Rebecca Bamber (8)
Our Lady of the Rosary RC Primary School

Kids

Kids are fun, kids are cool
Kids hang out in the swimming pool.

Kids are helpful, kids are lazy
But all of us are just plain crazy.

Kids are happy, kids are sad
But sometimes they can be quite mad.

Chey Lee (8)
Our Lady of the Rosary RC Primary School

Pets

P ets are such cute little things.
E ven though some do have wings.
T he cutest pet in all the land.
S ee it run across the sand.

Adam R Kelly (7)
Our Lady of the Rosary RC Primary School

Summer

S ummer is fun, summer is beautiful,
U nderneath the sand the beautiful shells lay,
M orning is here let's go and play,
M any people playing in the sand,
E aster next year, summer's still here,
R ise and shine morning again,
    off to the sea to swim in the waves.

Abby Shepherd (7)
Our Lady of the Rosary RC Primary School

Wings

If I had wings
I would touch the clouds
as they float around.

If I had wings
I would taste cheese
from the moon.

If I had wings
I would listen to the silence
of the fields of clouds.

If I had wings
I would smell the sweet
smell of Martian fields.

If I had wings
I would see the seven
wonders of the world
and dream of flying to all the planets.

Alex Owens (10)
Penruddock Primary School

The Door

Go and open the door,
maybe there's a castle with towering walls,
or a never-ending staircase.

Go and open the door,
maybe there's the fires of Hell, burning and bubbling,
or the tranquilities of Heaven.

Go and open the door,
maybe there's blank space,
or another door.

Go and open the door,
maybe there's a collapsing city, burning and crumbling,
or animals in a rainforest.

Edward Campbell (10)
Penruddock Primary School

Recipe For Autumn

Sift together some frost and smoke from a bonfire,
mix in coldness until dissolved.
Add a cupful of yellow, curled leaves
and throw a couple of woolly gloves and hats
into the bowl.
Stir the dissolved mixture until watery,
adding more frost if necessary.
Drop in a few oddly shaped conkers,
and Hallowe'en spirits.
Put into an old swallow's nest and
bake for three months on minus ten degrees.
Finally, brush with condensation until damp.

Katrina Gargett (10)
Penruddock Primary School

Autumn Thinkers

Crunchy leaves under the foot
And under the frozen moor
Sleep the hedgehogs under the earth
Will sleep for evermore.

Conkers inside a wicked shell
You think it might be mean
But under the horrid exterior
The smoothest of all seeds gleam.

All the autumn colours spin
With all the trees so brown and thin
Gold, red and orange too,
I think they are pretty, do you too?

Rachel Hogg (10)
Penruddock Primary School

You Are . . .

You are a cat,
lazing by the fire.

You are a sofa,
stretched out by the TV.

You are an old Beetle car,
broken down.

You are a sunflower,
bright and thin.

You are a trumpet,
loud and happy.

Chelsea Cartmel (10)
Penruddock Primary School

The Door

(Based on 'The Door' by Miroslav Holub)

Go and open the door,
maybe there's a unicorn
galloping by, with an angel
on its back.

Go and open the door,
maybe a star has fallen
on your step, and is twinkling
for you.

Go and open the door,
maybe a dragon is there,
with steaming breath and
bellowing fire.

Joanne Mitchell (9)
Penruddock Primary School

Open The Door

(Based on 'The Door' by Miroslav Holub)

Open the door,
maybe outside there's a magic tree growing -
it might grant you wishes.

Open the door,
maybe there's a group of monkeys
making a band.

Open the door,
there could be a ship
sailing silently by.

Don't open the door -
you will let a draught in!

Henrietta Leslie (9)
Penruddock Primary School

Wings

If I had wings
I would touch the furthest star.

If I had wings
I would listen to the heartbeat
of a jellyfish.

If I had wings
I would smell the sparks
from the biggest fireworks.

If I had wings
I would see Mercury
and count its moons.

If I had wings
I would taste a star
as it fell from the sky.

Sarah Lightburn (9)
Penruddock Primary School

Dinosaur

Reptile cheater,
meat eater.

Pack leader,
meat feeder.

Intestine spiller,
meat killer.

Dino dipper,
meat ripper.

Bone cruncher,
meat muncher.

Scent follower,
meat swallower.

Aidan Ford (8)
Penruddock Primary School

Wings

If I had wings I would
touch the moon and the sky.

If I had wings I would
taste the flavour of a flying cloud.

If I had wings I would
listen to the flap of a bird's wings.

If I had wings I would
smell the steam of the sun.

If I had wings I would
see the farmers rounding up their herds.

If I had wings I would
dream of dancing on the sun.

Lorna Pymm (10)
Penruddock Primary School

The Door

(Based on 'The Door' by Miroslav Holub)

Go and open the door,
there might be a witch, flying high up in the sky,
or a new world, waiting to be explored!

Go and open the door,
maybe you'll see wild horses roaming
in a distant land, a sparkling star, or even a ghost!

Go and open the door,
there may be nothing out there,
but still look and see.

Rachel Graham (10)
Penruddock Primary School

Recipe for Autumn

Sift together a handful of icy frost
with golden leaves,
mix in smooth, brown conkers.
Add a few sparks from a fierce bonfire,
leave until three months have passed.
Put into an old oak tree
and bake until crispy.
Finally, brush with a sprinkle of spines
from a hibernating hedgehog.

Bethanie Dixon (8)
Penruddock Primary School

If You Want To See A Tiger

If you want to see a tiger
you must go down to the muddy, slushy zoo.

I know a tiger
who's living down there -
he's a fierce, he's a mean, he's a shredding machine.

Yes, if you really want to see a tiger
you must go down to the muddy, slushy zoo.

Go down to that zoo and say,
'Tiger papa
Tiger papa
Tiger papaaaa.'

And down he'll come
But don't just stand there
Run for your life!

Anneka McCarthy (8)
St Bridget's RC Primary School, Egremont

If You Want To See A Tiger

If you want to see a tiger
You must go down to the muddy, slushy end of the Indian waterfall.

I know a tiger who's living down there
He's a shredding, a thrashing, a fighting machine.

Yes, if you really want to see a tiger
You must go down to the muddy, slushy end of the Indian waterfall.

Go down to the Indian waterfall and say,
'Tiger papa
Tiger papa
Tiger papaaaa.'
And you'll see him wake,
But don't get in a state,
Run for your life!

Kieran Raynor (7)
St Bridget's RC Primary School, Egremont

If You Want To See A Tiger

If you want to see a tiger
You must go to the yellow African grassland
I know a tiger who's living down there
He's a mean, fierce, fighting machine.

Yes, if you really want to see a tiger,
You must go to the yellow African grassland.

Go down to the grassland and say,
'Come here kit-cat
Come here kit-cat
Come here kit-caattt.'
And his head will rise,
But don't stick around,
Run for your life!

Benjamin Peacock (8)
St Bridget's RC Primary School, Egremont

If You Want To See A Tiger

If you want to see a tiger
You must go down to the muddy and dark jungle.
I know a tiger
Who's living down there -
He's a fierce, a big, a scary.
Yes, if you really want to see a tiger,
You must do down to the muddy and dark jungle.
Go down to the jungle and say,
'Tiger papa
Tiger papa
Tiger papaaaa.'
And up he'll rise
But don't look around
Run for your life!

Lara Kilgour (8)
St Bridget's RC Primary School, Egremont

If You Want To See A Tiger

If you want to see a tiger
You must go to the ooi gooi part of the jungle.
I know a tiger who's living down there -
He's a mean, he's a fierce, he's a shredding machine.

Yes if you really want to see a tiger
You must to down to the ooi gooi part of the jungle.
Go down silently to that muddy part and say,
'Tiger papa, tiger papa.'
And he'll slowly rise and growl
But don't stay for long
Run for your life!

Catherine Woodburn (8)
St Bridget's RC Primary School, Egremont

If You Want To See A Tiger

If you want to see a tiger
You must go down to the slushy, damp, icky swamp
at the end of the jungle.
I know a tiger
Who's living down there
He's a fierce, a mean, a tearing machine.
Yes, if you really want to see a tiger
You must go down to the slushy, damp, icky swamp
at the end of the jungle.
Go down to the bottom and say,
'Tiger papa
Tiger papa
Tiger papaaaa!'
And don't have a teddy bear's picnic
but
Run for your life!

Leona Byers (8)
St Bridget's RC Primary School, Egremont

If You Want To See A Tiger

If you want to see a tiger
You must go down to the muddy, slushy, rainy end of the jungle.
I know a tiger who's living down there
He's a mean, he's a big one, he's a wicked.
Yes, if you really want to see a tiger,
You must go down to the muddy, slushy, rainy jungle.
Go down to the jungle and say,
'Tiger papa
Tiger papa
Tiger papaaaa!'
And up he'll rise, but don't stick around
Run for your life!

Kaine Raynor
St Bridget's RC Primary School, Egremont

If You Want To See A Tiger

If you want to see a tiger
You must go to the wild animal park in Barrow.
I know a tiger
Who's living down there -
He's a brave, a big, and a meat eater.
Yes, if you really want to see a tiger,
You must go to the wild animal park in Barrow.
Go down to the wild animal park and say,
'Sly tiger
Sly tiger
Sly tigeeeeer.'
And he'll come out of the grass
But stay behind the fence.

Jack Hodgson
St Bridget's RC Primary School, Egremont

If You Want To See A Tiger

If you want to see a tiger
You must go down to the dull, sludgy and mucky jungle
I know a tiger
Who's living down there
He's a mean, he's a terror, he's a meat trimming tiger.
Yes, if you really want to see a tiger,
You must go down to the dull, sludgy and mucky jungle.
Go down into the dull sludgy and mucky jungle and say,
'Tiger papa
Tiger papa
Tiger papaaaa.'
And he will rise
But don't stay for even a chocolate digestive!

Tonicha Huck (8)
St Bridget's RC Primary School, Egremont

If You Want To See A Tiger

If you want to see a tiger
You must go down to the rainy, muddy end of the jungle.
I know a tiger who's living down there.
He's a mean, he's a fierce, he's an eating machine.
Yes, if you really want to see a tiger,
You must go down to the rainy, muddy end of the jungle.
Go down to the jungle and say,
'Tiger papa,
Tiger papa,
Tiger papaaaa!'
And he'll come but don't stick around
Run for your life!

Sophie Moran (8)
St Bridget's RC Primary School, Egremont

If You Want To See A Tiger

If you want to see a tiger
You must go down to the squelchy, rainy jungle.
I know a tiger who's living down there.
He's a fierce, an angry, a fighting machine.
Yes, if you really want to see a tiger,
You must go down to the jungle.

Fiona Herbert (8)
St Bridget's RC Primary School, Egremont

World's Creations!

The moon is shining,
The stars are twinkling
The leaves are falling everywhere
The world is going round and round
The birds are singing
The planet is growing, we should care.

Amy Warwick (9)
St Catherine's Catholic Primary School, Penrith

Why Don't You?

Why don't you
Stay in school?
Why don't you
Watch the sunrise?
Why don't you
Take a trip to the zoo?
Why don't you
Drink some chocolate in a mug?
Why don't you
Wrestle a sumo?
Why don't you
Go too?
Why don't you
Shout 'Shove!'?
Why don't you
Watch swans dancing?
Why don't you
Dance on the lake?
Why don't you
Have a cup of tea?
Why don't you
Go to sleep?
Why don't you
Watch The Simpsons?

Lauren De Klerk
St Catherine's Catholic Primary School, Penrith

All About Birds

I like birds
They're nice and fluffy.
I like birds
They are nice and lovely.
They like to flap their wings
And fly
And soar above the sky.

Katie Newton (8)
St Catherine's Catholic Primary School, Penrith

Seasons

Seasons come and go,
They never stop to say hello.
They always have to rush off,
They always come and go.
Seasons bring changes,
Some good, some bad,
Some make us happy,
Some make us sad,
Some make us hot,
Some make us cold,
Some make us shiver,
Some make us warm,
Some make us wet,
Some make us sweat,
Seasons come and go,
They never stop to say goodbye.
These are the seasons that have passed us by,
Spring, summer, autumn and winter,
Each and every one full of wonderful things.

Samantha Birkett (9)
St Catherine's Catholic Primary School, Penrith

Cars

They chatter, they bang
They turn, they skid
They smash, they crash
They're fast, they're slow
They're faster than a runner
Faster than a lion
They come in colours
They come in blue
They have speed
They're cars.

Xavier Lequitte (8)
St Patrick's School, Kendal

My Dad's Car

My dad's new car
Is a funny sort of thing.
It looks like a big yellow blob.
It goes chug, splutter,
Bang!

Chug, splutter, bang!
It's the most embarrassing
car
In the universe.
All my friends laugh at me
It's not very fast either
Last week its engine blew up.
My dad bought a Mini Cooper
Oh no! Here we go again!

Adam Laidlaw (8)
St Patrick's School, Kendal

Writing

You have to write slow
You have to write fast
It's really hard
Sometimes you're good at it
Sometimes you're not
Sometimes your hand hurts
You get confused
Sometimes you have to write a page or two
It's really boring
This is true.

Kelly Atkinson (8)
St Patrick's School, Kendal

Movement!

Horses gallop
Frogs leap
Cars go *beep, beep!*

Snakes swim
Babies gurgle
Runners go hurdle, hurdle.

Dogs bark
Penguins strive
Swimmers always have to dive.

Tigers growl
Cows trot
Cooks use a cooking pot.

Wolves howl
Cats stalk
Humans love a walk.

Mice run
Rats crawl
People do nothing at all.

I love swimming
And jumping too
They're the movements that I do!

Sophie Hodgson (9)
St Patrick's School, Kendal

Skeleton

It rattles chains and takes its head off,
It lives in a cave with the bats.

It clicks its bones and shakes its head,
It lives in the attic with the spiders.

Kieran Curwen (7)
St Patrick's School, Kendal

The Animal Alphabet

A lligators look like logs,
B ats sleep in the day,
C ats have sharp claws.
D ucks swim in the pond,
E lephants blow water out of their trunks,
F oxes live in dens,
G iraffes have long necks,
H ippos bathe in mud,
I guanas live in Mexico and Brazil,
J ays call harsh and loud,
K oala is like a cuddly toy,
L ion is the king of the jungle,
M onkeys swing from vines,
N ewts live in water.
O xen have thick coats,
P angolins curl up into tight balls,
Q uetzalcatlus is a prehistoric flying lizard,
R obins have red breasts,
S tarfish have five arms,
T arantulas are hairy,
U inta ground squirrels live underground,
V ultures are violent,
W alruses have plenty of fat to keep them warm,
X erus are rodents,
Y aks have horns,
Z ebras have black and white stripes.

Daniel Aldridge (8)
St Patrick's School, Kendal

Dance Moves At The Theatre

D rifting and dreaming
A bbie does acrobatics
N ice dances
C rawling and climbing
E asy and calm.

M akes me move
O ver and under
V ery special
E mma makes everything easy
S wirling and spinning.

A licia at the stage
T eacher shows me how to dance.

T ime is up
H urry my dance is coming
E asy to see me.

T ime to dance
H ere I am, look at me
E mma is dancing
A licia is rolling
T racy is twirling
R achel is spinning
E lla finishes.

Emma Winetrobe (7)
St Patrick's School, Kendal

Rabbits

R ound about the rabbit runs, racing through the flat black tube,
A lways twitching its fluffy, furry, soft, cute nose,
B ounding through the open air.
B iting carrots, *crunch, munch, gulp.*
I t's always alone, on its own, getting food and other things.
T rying hard to blend away,
S leeping in a soft, snug, warm burrow.

Hannah Kerigan (8)
St Patrick's School, Kendal

A Football Match

A ll the home crowd cheers when the team scores.

F antastic skills on the ball,
O n the ground they sing anthems,
O range balloons are thrown onto the pitch,
'T ake the free kick,' the referee says.
B eckham scores an absolute beauty for England.
A nthems are sung by international teams,
L iverpool are the best.
L imping when someone's hurt.

M ichael Owen scores a penalty for Liverpool,
A ll the away crowd 'boo' when a player gets sent off.
T en men are left.
C autions, foul!
H ackers kick people in the leg.
                    Penalty!

Sam Edward Portmann (8)
St Patrick's School, Kendal

Pony And Horse

P erfect mane flowing in the wind
O nly my pet, my true friend
N o one else loves him like I do
Y ou'd love him too if you knew him

A pples are his favourite food
N ibbles grass in his special field
D ancing in the summer sun

H ay is his winter fodder,
O ver the field he gallops
R eins guide him on the country roads
S unshine and showers, he's always here
E vening falls, another day tomorrow.

Hannah Robinson (9)
St Patrick's School, Kendal

Pink And Purple

P eople like pink,
I t is a skin colour.
N ow you know pink is white and red,
K eep pink for ever.

A nd pink is a colour that is red and white,
N ow you know how pink is made,
D o you know how purple is made?

P urple is a good colour,
U m! It is made from . . .
R ed and blue.
P urple is a good colour and pretty too,
L ovely warm colour,
E xcellent! So cool!

Georgia Wake
St Patrick's School, Kendal

What Rain Does

There's something coming from the white, fluffy clouds
Oh no! It is the rain
Splishing and sploshing down from the sky
Trickling down the icy pane
Making big deep puddles
Down the very muddy lane
There'll be flooding down in Kendal
It's not going down the street drain.
Quickly spilling into people's homes
Oh no! It is a shame.
The rain has left the houses.
The furniture is muddy
The cookers are broken
Oh dear! It's going to cost some money.

Laura Hunt (7)
St Patrick's School, Kendal

Dolphins

D olphins squeak and whistle
O cean breeze going from side to side,
L ining up for some food,
P eople ride on their backs.
H ow high can they jump?
I n the freezing cold water
N ear the beach,
S unny days are the best for me.

Jessica Beth Wake (7)
St Patrick's School, Kendal

Dolphins

D olphins are fun but they don't quack
O cean drifts up on their back
L ots of dolphins in the sea
P ouncing up when they look at me
H orses gallop but dolphins swim
I mpossible to see she's very slim
N icely diving I can see her
S he likes me very much and I like her.

Charlotte Bush (8)
St Patrick's School, Kendal

What Is It?

It's pittering and pattering on my roof
It sounds like a horse's hoof.
It drifts down one by one.
It's not like snow, it's faster than that.
It comes from the sky.
It's not a person, it's not a fly,
Something really heavy, it causes floods,
It can't be a drought.
   What is it?

Rachel Todner (8)
St Patrick's School, Kendal

Football In Malibu

Football is kicking a ball
Scoring a goal
That's all you need to do
With the football match at Malibu
All the goalies do is sit and play
With the cow from Malibu
Who can play football just like all of you
But I think he's better and greater
Than all of *you!*

Daniel Jones (8)
St Patrick's School, Kendal

Flying Things

The sky is for birds
But not for dogs because,
They don't have wings.
Pterodactyls are faster than dragonflies.
Some fish can fly.
Flying fish.
Butterflies are the best flying things in the world
There is a . . .
Kite that can fly.

James Mason (7)
St Patrick's School, Kendal

It's A Ghost!

The ghost lives in a spooky cave,
The ghost lives in a dark cupboard,
The ghost lives in a cold attic,
The ghost went into the car.
The man went into the car.
The man jumped out of the car . . . *Ahhh!*

Thomas Hankey (7)
St Patrick's School, Kendal

Things Animals Like

Cats like to purr
Dogs like to bark
Mice like to squeak
Birds have long beaks.

Snakes like to hiss
Monkeys like to swing
Tigers like to prowl
Lions like to growl.

Sharks like to bite
Jellyfish like to sting
Dolphins like to play
Whales like to spray.

Deer like to run
Squirrels like to climb
Hedgehogs like to hide
Swans like to glide.

Butterflies like to fly
Worms like to wiggle
Caterpillars like to crawl
Ants are so small.

Lori Colloby (8)
St Patrick's School, Kendal

The Sea

Crashing waves upon the rocks,
A sandy beach overhead,
Menacing winds undo the locks,
Swallowed sand on the seabed,
Darkened skies high above,
Clear blue waters below me now.
Upon the shore in lonely lands
Crashing waves upon the shore,
A sandy beach overhead.

Daniel White (10)
Sacred Heart School

Winter

Winter creeps up with a grin on his head,
He laughs at autumn for she is dead!
Rustling branches and killing off leaves,
In and out of people, he gently weaves.
Causing colds and spreading the flu,
Ready to strike either me or you!
He says, 'Bye, bye!' when spring comes,
He cannot stay, he has no chums.
Looming around, 'til next time,
So as he ends the year, I end my rhyme!

Grant Hamilton (11)
Sacred Heart School

The Night Sky

The darkness crept over the cottage,
The peeping moon peering,
The misty cloud shimmering,
The crimson sky glooming,
The glittering stars glowing,
The gloomy trees like fingers stretching to the peeping moon,
The flowers glistening,
The grass sparkling,
Although the house lay still.

Tania Butler (10)
Sacred Heart School

A Night Poem

The stars shine up at night
They shine a lot of light
Some shoot up, some shoot down
I don't know where they are found
They could be found on the ground
I don't know where they are found.

Kirsten Roberts (8)
Sacred Heart School

Remember

Remember when the sky was blue,
When all the children looked at the birds as they flew.
Remember when we ate some ice cream,
When we used to play and scream.
Remember when the sky turned grey
When all the children walked in dismay.
When you turn around the corner
All you see are troops, troops and more troops.

Joseph Fermoyle (11)
Sacred Heart School

Darkness

The darkness shimmered across the moonlit stream,
As the last glimmer of light shone like a beam,
The stars chased each other around the sky,
As the moon picked them up and said, 'Goodbye.'
The darkness fell slowly, slowly,
The light came up slowly, slowly.

Laura Taylor (11)
Sacred Heart School

The Fast Car

Flying through the streets,
Listening to the beats,
Overtaking cars,
The speed I'm going I could get to Mars.
I'm ready for a race
But nobody can catch up with my pace.

Cameron Gallagher (10)
Sacred Heart School

Up In The Attic

A cat's torn furry mouse,
My brother's scratched, battered sculpture of a rock,
My sister's rusty, scattered doll's house,
My dad's Victorian damp brass cuckoo clock,
A wooden splintered pine door,
My mam's ancient fractured china bowl,
Cracked picture frames lying on the stone floor,
My cobwebby blankets smeared in damp coal.
Up in the attic . . .

Kyle Dawes (10)
Sacred Heart School

A Night Poem

The night has come but not
Too soon, and sinking silent
All silent the little moon
Drops down behind the sky
The little moon is shiny and bright
It gives lots of light.

Milly Logan (9)
Sacred Heart School

Love

Love is in the air,
It is always there,
It is where you look,
Where you touch,
It is something
That we should share.

Charlotte Coote (11)
Sacred Heart School

The Dragon

The dragon, black hearted with fear
The dragon, cold and scaly
Its flame is as hot as a flaming pepper from beyond the top.
It is as tall as a skyscraper with legs,
It's the coldest thing, its scaly skin
Like one big shield or two
Its horn is as sharp as a razor with its mighty top
The dragon, the top of the food chain
With its curly horn for pain
The dragon which blows its mighty flames
Disposes enemies with a mighty blast of energy.

Philip Crompton (11)
Sacred Heart School

Football

Football the beautiful game
If you're good, you'll have plenty of fame
If you get a red, you'll be in shame
Join David Beckham and co.
But unlike him don't break a toe
Football the beautiful game.

William Young (11)
Sacred Heart School

School

Maths is first, it's under a curse
English second, that's how it's reckoned
Art is third, that's how it's heard
Geography forth, we learn about the north
PE fifth, we jump off a cliff
Last but not least, we have a great big feast!

Anne-Marie White (10)
Sacred Heart School

Winter

Winter is cold, wet and damp,
When I see puddles I love to stamp,
I love the frost, the ice and snow
It makes my face and fingers glow.

I love winter, it is fun,
We can make snowmen all day long,
We hear hats and scarves and mittens too,
But make sure you don't get a snowball
Thrown at you.

Snowflakes fall all around
They flutter gently to the ground,
How I wish it would snow
Then to school we would not go.

Alice Barnes (9)
Sacred Heart School

The Witch

Swooping, swaying through the sky
Looking down with a crooked smile
Glaring, staring with dusty eyes
An old ancient broom came out
Of a closet instead of a room
Twisted moles, with hairs sticking out
Knotted hair all scruffy and smelly
As she leaves something for everyone
A wicked cackle and a gloomy spell
Her chattering teeth and cold blue toes
Where she goes nobody knows.

Gemma Brown (10)
Sacred Heart School

NOS

I put my foot on the gas,
And I go really fast,
And my exhaust goes boom! Boom!
And then it goes blast!
And then I say to myself,
'I'm going to lose my garage,'
So I shove on the NOS
And I leave my cap in the past
And in the end I still own my garage.

Matthew Pickering (11)
Sacred Heart School

NOS

NOS, NOS I put my foot on the gas,
The clock goes up,
The NOS goes down,
I mean NOS,
I pump it all the time,
The muffler tip goes bang,
I used to have a skyline,
I thought I was good,
But it's just my car
NOS use it all the time!

Samuel Clayton (10)
Sacred Heart School

Wave At Me

I waved at the wave to see
If it would wave back at me,
But all I got is a wave,
Right back at me.

Joe Herbert (11)
Seascale Primary School

My Dad - Cinquain

Melvyn
Soft and gentle
Cooking in the kitchen
Snoring loudly whilst in his chair
Awake.

Louise Smith (11)
Seascale Primary School

Sarah's Lamb

Sarah's lamb went baa
And took off in a car
The car went hoot
And bashed the boot
So didn't get very far.

Sarah Huddleston (11)
Seascale Primary School

Turtle Cinquain

Turtle
a moving rock
a sunbathing swimmer
like a scrunched up, small piece of paper
Grandad.

Katie Linington (11)
Seascale Primary School

Snow

The snow creeps over land as a falcon hunting its prey,
Hurtling round, tree branches breaking,
Calms, calms, slowly drifts with birds soaring the skies.

Sadie Skivington (9)
Seascale Primary School

My Sister - Cinquain

Sister
Annoying girl
Can be kind, can be mean
Plays netball for the county team
Sophie.

Georgia Armstrong (10)
Seascale Primary School

My Dad Cinquain

Quiet
Sitting alone
As soft as a footstep
Like a pin dropping on the floor
Silent.

Rachel Borwick (11)
Seascale Primary School

Syllables - Cinquain

Work hard
Children playing
Teachers having a break
Eating at lunchtime next to friends
Home time.

Kellie Walker (11)
Seascale Primary School

Stormy Weather

The damp floor is still as a rock.
The lightning is loud.
The clouds are stormy and black.

Nathan Clark (9)
Seascale Primary School

Snow

She is frosty, she has a vast blanket over the earth,
She appears glittery and white,
Outside when she is around the air is freezing,
She is soft and crunchy, but she howls,
She melts gradually in the sun,
She covers the ground with a thick layer of white,
Which is icy and covers the earth.

Sarah White (9)
Seascale Primary School

Sea/See

I went to see the sea
And the sea didn't want to see me
But when I got there,
There was no sea to see me
It wasn't fair
I thought the sea didn't like me.

Matthew Thomas (11)
Seascale Primary School

Stormy Weather

A gust of wind passed my face,
Like a herd of elephants.
I stepped in a puddle,
Cold and damp
And we set up camp.
I lost my Wellingtons in the snow.

Luke McKerrow (9)
Seascale Primary School

Stormy Weather

It was on a summer night,
When the stars turned off
The music in my ears,
Suddenly everything was silent,
And the birds began to sing,
The moon was flashing
And the trees were,
And my heart was bashing,
And the sky was lit up with golden light,
And the thunder was bashing in.

Peter Maxim (9)
Seascale Primary School

Daddy - Cinquain

Daddy
Responsible
Nice, fun, warm and cuddly
Big, kind, friendly and quite funny
My dad.

Katie Dorward (9)
Seascale Primary School

Holidays

School hols
Children playing
The people at the swimming baths
People having ice cream and lollies
Great fun.

Lauren MacGregor (10)
Seascale Primary School

Stormy Weather

On a dark winter's night
Everyone sleeping,
Silent and still
With no fear
As a ferocious storm is near.
When everyone awakens
Children ready for school,
As soon as they step out of the door
Expecting sunshine . . .

Michael Krukowski (9)
Seascale Primary School

My Dad - Cinquain

Trevor
He's a great dad
He's got a very sore neck
He's a cop, oops the flowerpot
Clumsy!

Terrence Fail (10)
Seascale Primary School

Meteor Shower - Cinquain

Boulders
A crashing wave
Tan coloured striking rocks
Planets making red explosions
Comet.

Daniel McKerrow (11)
Seascale Primary School

Stormy Weather

The weather,
Rain tapping, tapping
On the window.
The wind in my face,
The puddles get deep in a short space of time.
A cloud crosses my hat.
The sea smashes at my knees.
The wind is soaring,
The people open the doors,
The boys and girls come out to play.

Thomas Jordan (9)
Seascale Primary School

Stormy Weather

Once it was a sunny day
But when the fast wind came
It was not the same.
I went outside
In the cold and damp rain
Without the blue sky
It was not the same.

Ryan Tallentire (9)
Seascale Primary School

The Guy From Peru - A Limerick

There once was a guy from Peru
Who dreamt he was eating a shoe
He woke with a fright
In the middle of the night
To find that his dream had come true.

Stuart Rigg (11)
Seascale Primary School

Stormy Weather

It started as a breezy day,
Then the wind picked up.

The rain trickled down my back,
The trees creaked, crackety crack.

The sky, dark and still,
With distant thunder crashing.

The fog is blinding my eyesight,
The wind, cold and icy bright.

The rain tearing down,
Making puddles all around.

The thunder is here now,
Bashing and crashing to the ground.

The stormy weather passing by,
Why did you send us the gloomy weather?

Why,
Tell me why?

Jane Eccles (9)
Seascale Primary School

Stormy Weather

One minute it is sunshine,
Next minute there is drips,
A minute passes.
Honking geese, migrating for winter.
Night and day I hear hail
Smashing on my windowpane.
Crash!
Bang!
Smash!
Slowly summer is ending,
Winter on the way.

Jake Saunders (9)
Seascale Primary School

Stormy Weather

It's a freezing cold day,
The lightning is bright yellow
And wet rain is its fellow.
The wind is blowing
And it is really annoying.

It's a freezing cold day,
The black, dull clouds are coming.
The thunder starts drumming,
The trees grow bare,
Whilst I just glare.

It's a freezing cold day,
As the fog comes down,
I put on my dressing gown,
Just as it said,
'It's time to go to bed.'

Callum Grant (8)
Seascale Primary School

Stormy Weather

The warm wind is dying on the ground.
The cold snow melting in the treetops,
There goes a tree, falling, falling.

The lightning; bright, golden, falling.
The thunder roaring its approval.
My house.

The sea is so, so, so ferocious,
The break waters have smashed.

There is so much rain, we're flooded,
We were hit by the flood
And lightning at the same time.
My mum's screaming,
That was the last thing I heard . . .

Jamie Bentley (8)
Seascale Primary School

Stormy Weather

I hate wind - fast and smooth,
Bashing and crashing - on the move.
Rain, rain hard and heavy
Dripping down windows and flowing slowly.

Lightning bright, lightning long,
Flashing as it lit up the sky
Like a disturbing song.

Misty mist, unsee-through now,
But I can still hear something,
It's hanging on two strings.
I can see it, it's . . .
Sparkling, it's . . .
The end!

Daniel Yetts (9)
Seascale Primary School

Stormy Weather

I saw the weather, it looked like bad weather.
It was the wettest and vilest rain ever.
Raging, roaring. It was really disgusting
And I was really sad.
Seagulls were flying with rage,
Thunder was really mad.

Thunder was booming and roaring,
It was fierce and loud.
Darkness. It was misty and full of fog with dark clouds.
Windy mists were picking up speed,
Wetness, darkness were light.
Crashing trees, lashing and bashing;
Smashing hailstones were hitting the ground with fright.

Luke Franks (9)
Seascale Primary School

Stormy Weather

The wind is howling with the trees blowing,
That is such a shame.
With the dark, grey clouds racing across the sky still,
That is such a shame.

The rain, wet and cold,
Running down my back, damp and pouring,
That is such a pain.
The fish are racing down the stream,
It's hard to catch them,
That is a pain.

Lauren Oaten (8)
Seascale Primary School

Stormy Weather

The rain is falling,
The leaves are pouring,
The day is boring,
The light is dulling,
Mist is growing,
The fierce rain is splashing,
Feeling stormy.

Nathan Rooney (9)
Seascale Primary School

Stormy Weather

The wind is scary and strong.
The rain is wet and soaking.
The river is noisy and fast.
The mist is cold and scary.
The leaves are falling off the trees.

Abbie N'Gale-Carrington (8)
Seascale Primary School

Jungle

Monkeys swinging in the trees,
Watching out for stinging bees,
Rattlesnake swirling round,
Listening for any sound,
Looking out from the top,
Looking for a tiny shop.
Falling down an elephant's trunk,
Listening for a tiny thump.
Swirling round in the blood,
Finding food for the good.

Eilidh Sproul (8)
Sedbergh Primary School

Deep Blue Sea

Jumping in the glistening water
whilst dolphins jump out to play.
Looking at the coral reefs,
swirling in the bottom,
whilst they hide in the reefs
from the big scary sharks.
The divers are getting little Nemo and Marlon.
They are as scared as a little mouse.

Bethany Orr (8)
Sedbergh Primary School

An African Safari

On the African safari it's as hot as an oven.
There are secret dragons which will get you
if you dare come out.
I saw a tiger that was red
with streaks of yellow lightning on his back.
I can see a giraffe as small as a Jaffa Cake.

Amy Bolsher (8)
Sedbergh Primary School

Mouse Attack

There was a mouse called Ravengskin
Every night he went in a bin.
He had a red tail and sharp little teeth
That ripped all the chicken and roast beef.
His ears were green and his fur was blue.
One day he did an awful poo!
It opened the bin lid and broke the door.
The next day the postman dropped a letter on his foot
It was red with blood.

Edward Pike (8)
Sedbergh Primary School

African Safari

In the African safari it's so sandy like a beach.
I would really have a peach.
Oh look, there is a lion with its long hairy mane.
Where's my Great Dane?
I can see a giraffe, as tall as the sun.
There's my Great Dane next to my other Great Dane.
Where's my freight train?
Oh there it is!

Zoe Jones (9)
Sedbergh Primary School

Polar Bears

Polar bears are as white as snow
They live in the Arctic and penguins do too
Polar bears can camouflage in the freezing white snow
Eskimos fish for seals then eat them raw
Walrus are really big and have enormous tusks
Polar bears can swim as fast as darts.

Thomas Rosenzweig (9)
Sedbergh Primary School

Under The Sea

The fish are as pink as a bed cover.
The sharks have very sharp teeth
As sharp as a nail.
I went down, down,
I saw an anchor as sharp as a knife.
I saw some divers diving in the sea!
I saw seaweed twirling like snow.
The fish are looking at me,
Will they dance?
There was a baby fish,
As little as a Jaffa Cake
I saw a treasure chest,
As yellow as the sun.

Natalie Milburn (9)
Sedbergh Primary School

Untitled

Once upon a rhyme
the cat got killed by swords of fire,
all because my hamster is a big fat liar.
I hid in a cave
what could be inside?
Yuk! It's the dead bride!
I hid in a house,
and squished a mouse!
Then I got found
and dropped a pound!
Once upon a rhyme!

Matty Goad (8)
Sedbergh Primary School

Under The Sea

Under the sea you can see fish,
Pirates and a lot more,
Like an underwater store.
Outside a lot more,
Go and see, you'll be surprised.
Down under the deep blue sea
Horses and a turtle
That's green and slow.
Sea horses orange, so bright,
Go and see in the deep blue sea.

Adam Roberts (8)
Sedbergh Primary School

Yu-Gi-Oh Dragons

The Tri-Horned Dragon has horns everywhere
The Metal Dragon is as hard as rock
The Crawling Dragon can't fly
The Lesser Dragon is as tough as a brick wall
The Darkfire Dragon is as hot as the sun
The Barrel Dragon is a mechanical dragon
The Pitch-Dark Dragon is as black as night
But Silfer the Sky Dragon
And The Winged of Ra rule them all.

Izaak Tyson-Hirst (9)
Sedbergh Primary School

Under The Sea

The coral is as sharp as a blade.
A shark's bite hurts like a bear trap.
The blue whale is heavier than three tonnes.
The dolphins jump out of the sea
Like a cheetah jumping up on a tree.

Simon Hunter (9)
Sedbergh Primary School

Animals

Cats, bats, are so fat,
They're as big as a mountain rat.
I've got a dog as big as a frog,
You have got a hog
That is like a log.
I've got a rabbit,
My rabbit can knit.
Animals, animals everywhere,
Animals going to see the bear.

Emma Postlethwaite (9)
Sedbergh Primary School

The Sea Animals

I went to the bottom of the sea.
On my way I met a shark
As grey as a rainy Thursday.

Then I met a fish as nice as a rainbow.

Then I went to the top of the sea.
I saw a bird so I went back down.

Then I met a fish as big as a tree.

Amy Thompson (9)
Sedbergh Primary School

Animals

Animals up and down, all around
Watch out, one is going to *shout!*
Animals that are small and tall
That are very small and that are very tall.
Animals that are sneaky and creepy
Oh, that was creepy!
Animals that are cute and loud.
That is loud!

Kristina Armitstead (9)
Sedbergh Primary School

Animals

The dolphin calls against a wall.
The baby dolphin has no fun.

The horse neighs when the owner waves.
The foal jumps when it sees a lump.

The rhino's horn is as beautiful as a unicorn.
The baby rhino isn't as big as you, I know.

Laura Woodfine (8)
Sedbergh Primary School

Animals

Once upon a rhyme,
a dog got killed.
A cat went miaow,
then the cow went moo,
the tiger went grrrr,
then the skunk went past,
and the elk got scared,
then the moth caught fright,
and all because
the dog that got killed.

Tom Cooling (9)
Sedbergh Primary School

Under The Sea

Divers look for treasure,
Sharks saying you don't have any
Pleasure boats in the sea,
All because of a shark the size of a pea.
Fish getting caught to go on dishes,
Sea creatures making water features,
Last of all plants wearing pants.

Lewis Harrison (9)
Sedbergh Primary School

Winter's Snowy Ice

W inter is cold and windy
I ce is slippery and fun
N ights are dark and windy
T o stay safe wrap up warm
E ver slipped on ice before?
R eady to run and have some fun.

S nowflakes fall continuously
N ow it's cold but fun
O n the snow I run, it crunches
W ind is loud and strong.

I ce is fun and slippery
C old and dark nights are coming so
E verybody wrap up warm
and keep safe winter's coming.

Hannah Stringer (9)
Warcop CE Primary School

My Baby Brother James

I've got a new baby brother,
he's called James White.
He's nine weeks old today,
and Mum says he's not crying as much at night.

James is starting to smile,
and makes a lot of noise,
and I've already started saying
he's going to get the best choice of toys.

James you've changed our life a lot,
but if somebody said
would I like to send you back
I'd say definitely not!

Bethany White (11)
Warcop CE Primary School

Imagination

I'm thinking of a creature,
I can't wait to meet ya.
In my imagination.

I'm thinking of a castle,
That does not want any hassle.
In my imagination.

I'm thinking of a wizard,
That is making a blizzard.
In my imagination.

Chelsea Venning (10)
Warcop CE Primary School

Midnight's Coming

Midnight's coming
The foxes come out.
The owls are hooting
Things are running about.

Sounds and thoughts
In my ears and head.
As I snuggle
Down in my bed.

Sam Pearson (10)
Warcop CE Primary School

In The Night

Owls hooting in the night
Scares me enough to put on the light.
A creak or a thump,
Makes a throat with a lump
And a thought with the thought
Of a kidnapper.

Hannah Hodgson (9)
Warcop CE Primary School

Night-Time Fright Time

When I am alone
In the middle of the night
I almost always get a fright
As the owl swoops low
The mice are squeaking
The floorboards are really creaking
Windows rattle
Bats take flight
In the middle of the night.

Elizabeth Koronka (10)
Warcop CE Primary School

Newts

I am a newt
I live in water
In a frosty pond.
It's as cold as can be,
I snuggle up warm.
Sometimes I go up the mountains to play.
I swim around all day,
But in winter
I stay and sleep
Under a soft rock.

Katie Bousfield (9)
Warcop CE Primary School

When The Dragon Learnt To Fly

When the dragon learnt to fly,
He flew so high in the sky,
He flew so high in the sky
He met the spirits and the gods
In the sky so, so very high.

Robert Shannon (11)
Warcop CE Primary School

When I Am Alone . . .

When I am alone
There are creepy shadows,
Strange noises,
A tingle in my toes.

Light shining off the roads,
Silent humming of animals and creatures,
'Oh no,' cry the mice
The fox has come to eat us.

Alone I am,
But soon it will be morning
The sun is dawning.

Kate Hayllar (11)
Warcop CE Primary School

If I Was A Tree

I would stand peacefully
Watching the world go by
Watching day and night.
Valleys are around me
Animals are around me
And children playing below me
As summer comes and goes
I stand watching throughout the seasons.

If only I was a tree.

Nikki Hughes (10)
Warcop CE Primary School

Mars

M ars is like a desert but with no life.
A nd no human has walked on Mars.
R ugged landscape makes it hard to travel
S ad as it seems there could have been life.

Thomas Balmer (10)
Warcop CE Primary School

When I Am Alone

When I am alone, I'm afraid,
When I am alone, I'm scared,
When I am alone, it's dark,
When I am alone, it's gloomy,
When I am alone, I hear noises,
When I am alone, it gets cold and creepy,
When I am alone, I can never get to sleep,
When I am alone, I'm sad,
When I am alone, it's scary
But I am never alone because I have
My family and friends.

Tom Ellis (10)
Warcop CE Primary School

Fish

Fish in the sea, swimming in the sea.
Under the rocks, away from the sharks.
The sun is out, dolphins jumping out of the water.
Boats swaying, catching fish, fish, fish.
Air coming out of killer whales.
Fish, fish, fish, fish.

Magan Simpson (10)
Warcop CE Primary School

Snow Time

Winter is a good time for snow
Icy roads cause accidents
Not good for children playing on icy roads
Time for children putting up the decorations
Everyone early to bed, next day the children
Unwrap their presents which are waiting for them.

Lauren Holmes (9)
Warcop CE Primary School

The Fuzzle

(Inspired by 'Jabberwocky' by Lewis Carroll)

In the dark depths of the sklie,
The gobbly goo did he lie,
With his great big glogs he heard a sound,
A sound in the distance; the fuzzle's gloud.

There he lay in his drave bed,
The king of fuzzles lay there dead,
He had managed to kill the gobbly goo,
But the gobbly goo's son killed him too.

In his will the king did put,
'Go and kill that great big smut',
Then one fuzzle did he say,
'I will make that gobbly goo's son pay.'

So did this fuzzle set off now,
To give the gobbly goo a kwupow,
So there he came to the gate,
The entrance to the thing he did hate.

The gobbly goo came out slow and said,
'You shouldn't have come, you'll soon be dead.'
But the little fuzzle stood up tall,
'You shouldn't have come, you great furry ball.'

The swords crashed,
The bodies got bashed,
Then the fuzzle laughed and said,
'Ha-ha, you're not that strong, you just lost your head.'

He dragged the head over his back,
He decided to put it in a big sack,
When he came back the fuzzles began to sing,
'Okio, we found our new king!'

Luke Parry (11)
Windermere Junior School

You'd Never Believe It

I would love to concentrate on listening
To the softness of my horse's fair mane on
A summer's evening.
I would love to breathe my horse's repeated
Heartbeat on a warm sunset evening.
I would dream of having a mouthful of the
Four powerful hooves thundering
On the rough road, when the moon is out.
I would slip away from the people
To hold happiness and gladness,
When I win the 1st place rosette
For my horse's show.

Kerri Hird (10)
Windermere Junior School

Impossible

I would like to scent the never-ending freedom
Of the mysterious golden eagle
I would like to stroke the power of a determined hunting pack of wolves
I would like to relish the spicy evil of the Devil
I would like to listen in on the forever silence of a single star
I would like to chorus a song with the soothing voices of the wind
I would like to steal the ferociousness of the beating drums of war
Keep it in my locket
To throw into the bottomless sea
I would like to catch the sympathy of a falling tear.

Megan Dean (11)
Windermere Junior School

The Chestnut Haiku

As white as fresh snow
Silk inside a chestnut shell
As soft as velvet.

Katrina Sheehan (11)
Windermere Junior School

I Wish Upon A Poem

I'd like to glimpse the sizzling and crackling of the squiggly noodles
As they're colliding with the starving tastebuds
On my begging tongue.

I'd like to catch a waft of the freshly fallen conker
On the leaf-strewn floor
On a cold autumn evening.

I'd like to overhear the smoothness of the rounders' bat
As I'm about to skilfully score a home run
Right around the field.

I'd like to investigate the cry of a puppy feeding
In its cosy mother's womb.

I'd like to flash a look at the hot gunpowder blasting its way
Out of its cartridge prison.

I'd like to catch the whiff of the skilful crow
Of the country-bound cockerel
Showing off in the warm summer's evening.

Alex Marsden (10)
Windermere Junior School

If Only?

I'd love to feel my guinea pig's soft squeaks and squeals
And the loud popping of popcorn
I'd like to taste the smell of roasting potatoes in the oven

Or to taste the sensitive texture of a velvet dressing gown
I'd love to eat a chunk of the sun and
Taste its peppery hotness on my tongue
I'd love to listen to sugar and lemon pancakes freshly made

I'd like to steal the moon's icy rays and keep them in my pocket
I'd love to capture the sun's soul and keep it beautifully in a jar

I'd love to snatch the spirit of a great oak tree and keep it in my heart
I'd love to paint the butterfly's last breath and keep it forever more.

Charlotte Wragg (10)
Windermere Junior School

Growking Gronc

(Inspired by 'Jabberwocky' by Lewis Carroll)

A restless soul loofed along,
Sounding like a goopy klong,
Crumping, blanging about the flonc,
Groaring, plamming did the gronc,

No one cared about the gronc,
No one cared he had the scronc,
But blurky and blubbery really he was,
Upset and alone like a big stig bloz,

But one day came a bailing sight,
A giflomae shot in to fight,
Breathing frice and smashing down walls,
Speefing up and spitting balls,

A cry of terror the gronc just heard,
So quickly dreeping through the mird,
He picked up his old trusty splail,
And gallumphed through the spoofing gale,

Down the mountain, through the grook,
Across the smomp, and past the mook,
Until the gronc had made its way,
To the blamming, blomming giflomae,

They battled, they spattled their weapons raised high,
Then the gronc flunked up to the sky,
Down he came with a bom and a bam,
The giflomae was flattened to sham,

So from then on everyone cared,
They brought him splop and brought him flared,
And the gronc was then known as growking gronc,
For all he had done and saving town blonc.

Charlie Cook (10)
Windermere Junior School